No!
I Don't Have
15 Minutes to Chat

What Top Tech Execs Wish
Salespeople Knew About Getting in the
Door and Earning the Business

DAVID SILVERSTEIN
and RANDY GABORIAULT

Wayne, PA

SellingtotheCIO.com
260 Kerrwood Drive
Wayne, PA 19087
sellingtothecio@gmail.com
www.sellingtothecio.com

Ordering Information: Special discounts are available for bulk purchases. To inquire, please email the publisher or visit our website.

It's So Easy
Participation Pays Off
LinkedIn Is Not a Dating Service
Discover First, Prescribe Second
Get Attention the Right Way!
It's Meeting Time. Use It Wisely
Are You a Frog or a Good Relational Seller?
Salesperson or Stalker: What's the Difference?

Project Manager: Marla Markman, www.marlamarkman.com
Cover and Book Design: Kelly Cleary, kellymaureencleary@gmail.com

ISBN Print: 978-1-7345684-0-0
ISBN e-Readers: 978-1-7345684-1-7
ISBN: Audiobook: 978-1-7345684-2-4

Printed in the United States of America

CONTENTS

Foreword

WHEN YOU THINK OF TECHNOLOGY, your first thought could be of innovation, transformation or automation. This $5 trillion industry is revolutionizing the world we live in and the way global business is being done. However, what doesn't get discussed much—if at all—is the art and science of how technology is bought and sold.

For such a transformative industry, very little time is spent studying the art of selling technology solutions. It is a complicated and competitive market where today's technology winners are tomorrow's also-rans. So how can you be confident in what you are selling while ensuring strategic alignment with your customer's goals and objectives? Answering this question is essential if you are to be a successful technology salesperson.

It takes years to master the various subtleties of sales, whether from an IQ or an EQ perspective. Deep knowledge of the tech industry and products must be meshed with the skill of understanding people and immersing yourself in your customer's situation as they entrust you with their success or failure. Make no mistake, if a CIO makes a wrong purchase decision in today's "winner take all" business environment, it can not only jeopardize the project and the business, but also their livelihood.

In the chapters ahead, you will get a range of insights from both sides of the table on what it takes to be a successful technology salesperson in today's ever-changing world. The feedback shared by both salespeople and CIOs will provide valuable insights into how one gains access to the CIO, how to properly prepare for that important meeting, how to build relationships and the secrets to sealing the deal. Absorbing this inside perspective will help you to better customize your sales approach and become more strategic with your customers.

The art of sales has been discussed and debated for years. Some people say that you are either born a good salesperson or not. I disagree. Sales it is a skill that can be continually nurtured, honed and sharpened. The firsthand experiences shared in this book reveal the nuances you must navigate to fine-tune your capabilities and become a successful technology salesperson.

Enjoy and happy selling.

Michael Friedenberg

President, Reuters

Introduction

WHEN SALESPEOPLE AND CIOS WORK TOGETHER, great things can happen. The co-authors of this book are a case in point. When veteran salesperson David Silverstein and CIO Randy Gaboriault got to know each other, they began talking about their experiences from both sides of the trenches. The pair quickly realized they had the makings of a book—this book— on their hands.

But unlike every other sales book you've ever read, this one isn't full of tips from successful salespeople. Instead, we went straight to the source—CIOs themselves—to gather insider insights on what works and what doesn't when selling to them. After all, who better to advise you on selling to CIOs than the very people you're targeting?

This book compiles the wisdom of dozens of CIOs in a wide range of industries, from financial services and technology to law and health care. We talked to CIOs of both private companies and publicly traded firms, midsized companies and multinational organizations.

Although the stories in this book are anonymous, all the CIOs behind them are real. Each generously shared pet peeves and war stories about how salespeople try to sell them—and what they wish salespeople would do instead. We've also included perspectives from successful salespeople who share their battle-tested tactics for getting through to the CIO, setting the meeting and making the sale.

"Fewer than one in a thousand salespeople gets it right," one CIO we spoke to told us. This book will help you beat those odds. Selling is hard; it takes a lot of "No's" to get to "Yes." But when you employ the techniques in this book, you'll begin to build relationships with customers that go beyond the transactional. Instead of just a salesperson, you'll become a trusted partner that your customers will rely on.

Do you want your customers to consider you a friend and a resource? Do you want to be the kind of salesperson whose customers follow you from company to company? Take the lessons in this book to heart, and you'll be on your way to earning that kind of loyalty.

CHAPTER 1

Making
the Connection

EMAIL, TEXTING, SOCIAL MEDIA, VOICEMAIL—with so many ways salespeople can reach out and touch CIOs, shouldn't it be easier than ever to make that initial connection with a new prospect? In reality, with so much "noise" out there, connecting with a CIO for the first time has gotten more challenging, not less.

In this chapter, you'll learn real-life success strategies and tips to help you break through the barriers and make initial contact with a CIO. We'll also share CIOs' pet peeves, the most common mistakes salespeople make when trying to get through the CIO's gatekeeper, and the tactics that will earn you a permanent place on any CIO's blacklist.

Want to be one of the chosen ones whose calls actually get connected to the CIO? Keep reading.

What *Not* to Say to the CIO's Gatekeeper

For an executive assistant (EA) like me, each day presents an exciting new challenge and opportunities to learn.

What do you learn?

As the gatekeeper to a CIO, I quickly learned that sales calls come in constantly and that no matter how you respond to a request, whether by phone or by email, salespeople keep pressing on, rarely taking no for an answer.

I learned that I needed to "up my game" after I allowed a piece of correspondence to get past me (the gatekeeper) and onto my C-level boss's desk. It was a nicely packaged, neatly handwritten note thanking my boss for accepting her invitation on LinkedIn. This led me to believe my boss had a relationship with this person.

I soon found out that wasn't true. That also taught me this salesperson was trying to establish a relationship with my boss, and our organization, based on a lie. No integrity, no ethics, no bueno.

Or consider the caller who politely introduced himself as my boss's cousin Brian. Since I hadn't known my boss very long, I wasn't yet attuned to his family. You guessed it: There was no such person in his family.

One of my all-time favorite calls requested my boss clear his calendar to meet with a company and see its amazing product...at the request of Ted Kennedy. Knowing that Senator Kennedy had passed away in 2009, I was immediately suspicious. Turns out "Ted Kennedy" is a fairly common name (unfortunately, so is this bogus sales tactic).

Here are some of the most common lies I have heard sales folks tell in an effort to beat the system and get past the gatekeeper:

- "It's a personal matter."
- "I've worked with or spoken to X from your organization

who referred me to your boss."
- "I'm calling on behalf of the CEO of X company."
- "I just need a few minutes of his time."
- "I met him at [name of conference]."
- A gross mispronunciation of the exec's name.
- His first name. If you know him so well, why don't you have his mobile number or direct line?
- "I am your new account executive." Then why didn't the previous account executive leave you my boss's direct contact information?

So how do you get past the gatekeeper? There is no magic formula—but there's a simple one: Be honest and be nice.

I realize you are working from a script: your goals, what or whom you represent, what you have to offer, why your solution works better, yada yada. You're in this for the long haul until you get the desired outcome: a meeting. I can help if you treat me the right way—with respect. Here are some suggestions for doing that.
- Do thank me.
- Don't be pushy.
- Do know the difference between persistence and annoyance.
- Don't bully me or use derogatory techniques to shame me into thinking I'm "only a secretary."
- Do know all calls to my boss are handled and triaged by me. If you do not feel comfortable talking to me, I cannot share your message with my boss.
- Don't underestimate what I know about my department or my organization.
- Do tell me why you're calling. It may be more appropriate that your call goes to another member of our leadership team.

—*The Gatekeeper*

THE TAKEAWAY

Remember, I stand beside my boss, not behind them. They rely on me to screen their calls. I'm a strong, confident partner. Treat me as such. Be honest with me. That's what sells—and what just might get you the meeting.

GETTING TO KNOW YOU

Without the CIO's administrative assistant on your side, you're sunk! Do yourself a favor and spend the necessary time getting to know these folks. They hold the key to getting meetings (not to mention any other information you are looking for). Treat admins like gold, and give them the same respect you would their managers.

Respect My Admin

Another of one of "those" calls came into my assistant (let's call them Patience) recently, and I got to eavesdrop on it.

Caller: Hi, I'm Joe from Techno Corp. calling for Mr. CMIO.

Patience: Can I tell him what you are calling about?

Joe: I am calling for my managing director, and I am only allowed to talk to Mr. CMIO. I am not allowed to tell you why we are calling.

Patience: Mr. CMIO will only take your call if I can tell him who is calling and why.

Joe: It's between Mr. CMIO and my managing director, and it's none of your business.

Patience, slightly annoyed and insulted, sends Joe to voicemail so he can leave a message that I will promptly delete.

Pulling rank on the administrative assistant is a ridiculous sales tactic on several levels and pretty much guarantees your attempt to reach the CIO will fail. Let's break down why this approach is so bad:

- *My very talented administrative assistant is screening the calls exactly the way I want them to.* They have my complete trust and know me well. They also own my calendar. As a caller trying to get to me, you have no choice but to play the game. Annoy my assistant and I will never know you exist. I like it that way.
- *The caller is an "appointment setter" trying to set up a meeting for their mythical managing director.* The idea that the appointment-setting caller will only talk to the CIO implies, with the subtlety of a sledgehammer, that the managing director of the vendor views himself and his time as more important than the CIO of the client. Thanks for the insult, now go away.
- *Almost nobody (except the CEO and my wife) gets through*

5

to me directly. I am very busy; I get 50 phone calls a day; and most days, my calendar is full. If you don't have a clear reason to call and talk to me and/or an appointment, you will never get connected.

- *If there is truly confidential information to be shared, I would have set up another channel to communicate.* My admin knows this (they know everything). Don't treat them this way.

I don't blame Joe for his approach. I blame his boss (the great and mighty managing director) for setting him up to fail.

THE TAKEAWAY

To get to me, you must always deal with my administrative assistant. Don't annoy and insult either of us. When you pull rank, you are sending a message as to how you treat junior people—and how you treat *my* people. Basic courtesy goes a long way.

8 Ways to Get to (and Through) the Gatekeeper

As a young sales professional decades ago, I would open my *Rand McNally* map book every morning to target where I wanted to spend my time that day. Back then, we had no digital tools—not even email—to rely on for sales prospecting. Rather, we would drive to an office park and cold call on prospects door-to-door.

On one occasion, I vividly recall walking into a law office where I immediately encountered the "gatekeeper." Before I could introduce myself, she was calling security to escort me from the building. My crime? Solicitation and trespassing.

At that point in my career, I've been asked to leave a building, but had never had someone get security to walk me outside and tell me never to come back. Upon returning to my office later that day, I was still furious that someone took it that far.

I decided to do something born more out of trying to make her feel guilty than commencing a sales cycle: I sent her a handwritten note apologizing for intruding on her day.

Unexpectedly, the gatekeeper called me that day to apologize for her extreme behavior. A conversation ensued, concluding with us scheduling an introductory meeting.

This innocuous moment early in my career made me understand the significant role gatekeepers play before, during and after a sales cycle; appreciate the critical need to develop a pitch specific to this role; and embrace the process of developing a relationship with executive assistants. With this background in mind, here are eight best practices for managing the person who stands between you and the CIO.

1. *Acknowledge gatekeepers to their boss.* They have a hard job, so acknowledging them to their manager isn't just the

right thing to do, but it also shows that you appreciate and care about them.

2. *Build trust.* This part of the relationship is a journey, so it takes time and many small steps, but the payoff is tremendous. One way to build trust is to make the gatekeeper part of the team, even though they'll never participate in a meeting or demo. One of my favorite things to do is to schedule my first meeting as a "lunch and learn." I always order more food than we need and make it a point to bring a few options to the gatekeeper before the meeting starts to thank them for helping me organize the meeting. I let the gatekeeper know that even though they're not in the room with us, I consider them to be part of the team and I value their time, effort and energy.

3. *Don't waste the gatekeeper's time.* I don't know about you, but I hate when people waste my time—and gatekeepers do, too. When you make your initial call, don't engage in small talk. Have a gatekeeper-centric "elevator pitch" that is tailored to the gatekeeper's (and their manager's) role.

4. *Provide value.* I'll do just about anything if there's value associated. So will a gatekeeper.

5. *Don't ask questions to which you could easily learn the answers by doing your own research.* Speaking of research, learn as much as you can about the organization, its strategic initiatives, its executives and, yes, the gatekeeper. They, too, have a digital footprint. Start with LinkedIn, Facebook and Instagram. Sometimes a simple search on Google will yield some very interesting nuggets that you can leverage in your initial conversation with a gatekeeper.

6. *Speaking of social media, gatekeepers generally aren't monitoring their managers' social media accounts.* However,

engaging CIOs directly through LinkedIn, Twitter and other social media sites must be done cautiously. Your prospect probably gets hundreds of invitations to connect on LinkedIn each week. Instead, use LinkedIn or other social media accounts to glean information about your prospects that you can use to make a connection. Perhaps you share common interests, such as supporting women in STEM occupations or volunteering with inner-city children. Do you know the same people? If so, approach your connection to see if you can get a "warm" referral to the prospect.

7. *Find a link.* Often, there are two degrees of separation between you and a stranger. Find a common acquaintance who knows the gatekeeper and ask for a referral. Getting a warm introduction to the gatekeeper will make it easier to get to your primary target.

8. *Get a referral.* If your gatekeeper works for a VP, start by reaching out to the gatekeeper for the CIO. Chances are the CIO's gatekeeper will shut you down. When they do, ask them if it's OK to call the VP's admin. A top-down, gatekeeper-to-gatekeeper referral can be very effective.

Gatekeepers, especially C-level executive assistants, are some of the most knowledgeable people in the entire company. From understanding the mission of the CEO and how the CIOs will execute; from the company culture to the personalities of the executives; from corporate rumors and gossip to unpublished facts, gatekeepers *know things.* Taking the time to build relationships with them will pay off big time.

As for the gatekeeper who tossed me out of her building years ago, she moved to another company shortly after our first encounter. One of her first acts in her new role was to call me to schedule a meeting with her new manager. In the end, she became a friend and mentor. She's retired now, and I miss her dearly.

THE TAKEAWAY

Building a relationship with the executive assistant or other gatekeeper is just as important as building a relationship with the CIO. Don't think of the gatekeeper as an obstacle to get past; think of them as a person to connect with.

THE BIG 3

Three things guaranteed to get you on every CIO's do-not-call list?

1. Asking them if they have 10 minutes to explain their needs to you. It's your job to know their needs.

2. Sending the same cold email every day . . . for eternity.

3. Bombarding them with LinkedIn messages the minute they accept you as a connection.

What Would the CIA Do?

What's in a name? Quite a lot. As a CIO, salespeople who grab my name out of thin air stand out among the bad, the ugly and the downright foolish sales strategies I encounter every day.

I've received countless numbers of pitches like these:

1. "You are listed as the CIO of [insert my employer's full legal entity name, not the name everyone refers to in the real world. Instead of 'ABC Corp.' they say, 'ABC Corporation of America']."

2. "Your name was given to me."

3. "I came across your name."

4. "Your name was referred to me as someone I should speak to."

5. And the number-one offender: "I saw your name."

These pathetic attempts to sell are not only ineffectual but also deeply naive. They reflect both a lack of sales experience and a lack of understanding of the CIO and what their offering means in the context of the CIO's universe.

Such offenders are rarely prepared to respond when I ask a simple question about their opening statement, such as "Who referred you?" Not being able to answer that question is a sure-fire strikeout.

Successful sales efforts require what I call "relationship connectivity," and that requires a strategy that fits into context.

Think of it this way: If the CIA were seeking information on a target, how might they strategize and start building relationships?

Likely, they begin with an inventory of known information and start by working indirectly and iteratively closer and closer, until they're ready to directly (and effectively) engage with the target.

THE TAKEAWAY

You're not a magician, so stop grabbing names out of thin air. Instead, approach your sales goal with the same investigative power and focus the CIA would use to accomplish a mission.

THE BEST GIFTS
DON'T COME IN A BOX

Salespeople waste a lot of money sending CIOs gifts without knowing how the CIOs feel about getting them. My favorite kinds of gifts are intellectual gifts. That could be an ebook or a white paper that aligns with a topic of interest to me—anything that educates me and intrigues me enough to get me to ask questions. As a CIO, I don't have time to understand all the solutions out there. Something that's targeted and helps me understand has real value—unlike all the junk gifts I get in the mail.

What Part of "No" Don't You Understand?

For weeks, the same telecom audit vendor has been calling me almost hourly and emailing nearly as frequently with promises to save me 250% on my monthly phone and data bills. These calls persist despite email requests to cease and desist, attempts to unsubscribe from the mailing list, and my admin getting flat-out rude about it. It's a different sales rep almost every time, but the pitch is always the same.

Finally, in desperation, I decided to answer the phone myself. When the rep kicked into his pitch, I stopped him cold with a demand to cease this unprofessional and unethical assault on our phone and email systems. I also threatened to block their phone number and email domain if the assault continues (ah, the perks of being CIO!).

He proceeded to tell me that the only way I can get off their contact list is by having an in-person meeting with their CEO and my CFO.

I nearly broke the phone hanging up. And yes, I blocked their phone number and email domain.

It turns out that my CIO peers knew exactly who I was talking about when I told them my story; I never even had to mention the company name. If we all despise your tactics, no wonder you have to work so hard to get any business.

What part of "no" don't they understand? Rotating sales reps, bombarding me with multiple calls and emails a day, and refusing to respect my requests will only anger me; it will never result in business. This approach is every negative sales stereotype coming to life. It makes legitimate salespeople look bad.

Even my kids know when to stop asking. Remember: No means no. And eat your vegetables.

THE TAKEAWAY

Persistence is a virtue—but only up to a point. Don't cross the line from persistent to pest.

What's the worst way a salesperson tried to get through to you?

"I got a golf club. It wasn't cheap. I'm not a golfer. They never got a meeting."

"Invitations from salespeople I've never met to attend a ball game or other local event I have no interest in."

"They said, 'I golf at the same club as your CEO. Do you want to keep your job?'"

"They said, 'If you don't buy our product, we'll ensure you get audited.'"

"They lied. CIOs share insights, so if you're dishonest, they'll find out."

"I had a security firm send me something in the mail on an unencrypted thumb drive."

"A publicly held software company sent me, the CIO of a publicly held company, a $100 bill in the mail. It wasn't Monopoly money, either."

"When people scold me for being rude by not getting back to them. It gets my attention, but in a bad way."

"They claimed to be my cousin. Why would you want to start a relationship with a lie?"

"The unknown salesperson used my email address to send me calendar invites for a meeting and a series of webinars, which put a weekly recurring event on my calendar."

How Would You Treat a CIO?

How would you seek to do business with a CEO? Would you have a different approach for the CEO of a startup, a $1 million firm, and a $500 million firm?

In any of these cases, would you ever call the CEO's office and leave a voicemail message announcing you will be "in the area" next week and want to "stop by" to introduce yourself?

Would you have an inside sales rep call the CEO on behalf of "Person X, our vice president" and say, "X is going to be in your area next Tuesday and would like to stop by for a few minutes to discuss our offering"?

Of course not. This is a ridiculous approach. So why on earth do salespeople use it with CIOs?

I suspect this technique originated in the 1980s. It worked for one copier salesperson, he taught it to others, and it spread like a virus to other organizations.

Even if this approach worked in the '80s, today it's about as appropriate as leg warmers and acid-washed denim. (For the young sales reps reading this, those fashions were cool back then.) It demonstrates a lack of sophistication, reveals complete ignorance of how your prospect organization operates, and shows you don't understand how others use their time.

Here's an example of a real voice mail that was left at my office this week. (Names and numbers have been changed to protect the guilty).

Hello, this is Chip S. from ABC Consulting. We are an IT staffing and consulting company and I was going to be in your area next Tuesday and Thursday and wanted to know if I can stop by and introduce myself and see what possible needs you may have in the coming month. Please give me a call when you have the opportunity. 555-1212, extension 270; 555-1212, extension 270. Thanks in advance for your time.

Making a bad approach worse, Chip delivered the obviously scripted pitch poorly. His speaking cadence was unnatural, full of pauses, stops and starts completely unrelated to sentence structure or normal human speech.

Chip did not receive a call back.

THE TAKEAWAY

Don't ask the CIO to bend to your schedule. Show that you value our time.

Cut and Paste Just Doesn't Cut It

A sales rep from a very large software company copied and pasted a piece of my bio from our website into the email she sent me.

The bio clearly states that I am the company's CIO and head of IT. The rep's email gushed about how inspiring my bio was and how much she wanted to meet me and tell me all about her company's software. Then she asked if I could I introduce her to the head of IT.

People, please read and reread your own "form emails" so they don't make you sound stupid. Poor use of copy and paste doesn't cut it. My delete key was the only response.

THE TAKEAWAY

Spend a few minutes proofreading your emails before you hit Send.

What You Think Makes You Different Just Makes You the Same

Today was a good day. I only got 25 emails from companies I've never heard of. The funny thing is that they all say the same things about themselves.

Here are some points that each of these firms call out as distinctive differentiators for their businesses. Enjoy!

We are proud to be a Certified:

- Microsoft Gold Development Partner
- Oracle Gold Partner
- HP Silver AllianceONE Partner

These partnerships combined with our industry experience allow us to help our clients make key business decisions across multiple technology platforms.

We offer:

- expertise in the Microsoft Stack (WSP, ASP.Net, C#), Java/JEE, SAP, Oracle SOA/SOA Fusion as well as Mobile, Business Intelligence (Big Data) and Share-Point, and Cloud Deployments (SAAS)
- IT consulting, IT staffing and IT support services
- implementation and optimization service

Our mission:

- is to deliver high-quality software on time, on scope, and on budget
- is to ensure your requirements are met and exceeded

We provide:

- industry experts to work directly on-site with our customers
- cutting-edge high-quality software solutions to meet enterprise business needs

We have:

- a customer-centric approach

- a proactive recruiting methodology
- a strong sense we can have real impact

We are:

- completely devoted to being the number-one company in improving organizations
- low cost
- nimble
- growing

Miscellaneous:

- Our capabilities empower CIOs to deliver solutions that delight their business users.
- Our model is tailored to be as economical as possible for enterprises at scale.
- If you're not leveraging this data, you're missing out on the strategic opportunities that your competition is already enjoying.

The good thing is, each one only wants 15 minutes of my time, and they all look forward to hearing from me!

THE TAKEAWAY

Meaningless marketing jargon won't convince prospects to talk to you—especially if it just repeats what your competitors are saying. Instead, lead with what you have done in my industry. That gets my attention.

Remember Me?

I am very protective of my time. Time is neither infinite nor expandable, so I do not speak to salespeople who are just looking for conversation. My executive assistant is careful in making calendar decisions: She knows what is important and what is not important for my time allocation.

So far this week I have received two emails from "Rick" in as many days (and it's only Tuesday). Here they are (identities have been changed to protect the guilty).

Email #1: Monday, June 17, 11:13 am

Mr. CIO,

I am not sure if you recall, but we spoke briefly back in Q4 of last year. The ABC Group is a leading Strategy and Operations Management Consulting firm. We help clients reduce their costs, grow their top line, and transform their organizations through designing and implementing scalable and repeatable solutions. My SVP would like to introduce himself and The ABC Group to you as well as our extensive experience within IT. Is there a day over the next few weeks where you have a window for a very brief 30-minute conference call?

I'd be more than happy to work with your assistant to arrange a mutually convenient date and time. No timetable to do business—just introductory. I look forward to hearing from you soon.

Best regards,
Rick

Email #2: Tuesday, June 18, 4:15 pm

Mr. CIO,

I wanted to circle back you. I sent an email to you this past Sunday afternoon in regard to hoping to get a few minutes on your calendar for a very brief call. We spoke briefly back in Q4 of last year. The ABC Group is a leading Strategy and Operations Management Consulting firm. We help clients reduce their costs, grow their top line, and transform their organizations through designing and implementing scalable and repeatable solutions. My SVP would like to introduce himself and the ABC Group to you as well as our extensive experience within IT. Is there a day over the next few weeks where you have a window for a very brief 30-minute conference call? The dates below are our availability for July. Please list a date and time that best fits your schedule and we will work around them. All times are in Central time zone (CST).

7/2 OPEN
7/3 OPEN
7/4 10:30-5:00
7/5 9:30-2:00
7/8 10:30-1:00, 3:00-5:00
7/9 11:00-1:00, 3:00-5:00
7/10 OPEN
7/11 10:00-5:00
7/15 9:00-1:00, 3:00-5:00
7/16 11:00-1:00, 3:00-5:00
7/17 OPEN
7/18 10:00-2:00
7/19 9:30-1:00
7/22 11:00-1:00, 3:00-5:00
7/23 OPEN
7/24 OPEN
7/25 10:00-4:00
7/26 8:00-1:00, 3:00-5:00
7/31 OPEN

I'd be more than happy to work with your Executive Assistant to arrange a mutually convenient date and time. No timetable to do business—just introductory. I hope to hear from you soon.

Best regards,

Rick

Besides the explicit absurdity in his approach to calendaring, Rick is an outright liar.

I've never spoken to or met Rick before, and I never will.

I find it very interesting how many salespeople claim to have worked with me or to have spoken to me and, subsequently, tell me (and others) that they have done so!

Rick has polluted the water for the rest of you. Salespeople like Rick are destroying the brands they represent and creating a culture of deceit and mistrust. They owe us all an apology.

THE TAKEAWAY

Don't lie—especially about knowing the person you're lying to.

She's No Friend of Mine

I arrived at the office yesterday to find a letter on my desk. It had been carefully removed from its envelope by my assistant, who placed it front and center.

Everything on the envelope, including the return address, was handwritten in a smooth, flowing cursive that reminded me of my childhood schoolteachers' penmanship. It looked like a personal letter, the kind only my mother would still send.

Boy, was I intrigued. Why was this letter on my desk? My assistant serves as a tremendous gatekeeper, removing a vast number of sales attacks from ever reaching me. This letter must be something very important to have passed my assistant's screening test and get put directly in my flight path to intentionally earn a moment of my time and attention.

I scanned the letter. It was typed and was immediately identifiable as a sales letter, done as a basic mail-merge with my name and company inserted at predictable spots, and hand signed by one Karen L.

I was baffled. Why was this letter on my desk and not in the recycling bin?

Then I read the first line: *I wanted to thank you for accepting my friendship on LinkedIn and very much appreciate your response to my email.*

Now I knew why that letter was on my desk. Based on that sentence, my assistant concluded that Karen and I had an established relationship and decided to pass the letter on.

There was just one hitch in the chain of success that Karen had achieved in her business development journey to reach me:

That opening statement had not a shred of truth in it.

I was not connected to Karen on LinkedIn, nor had I ever exchanged email correspondence with her.

Well done, Karen! You and your employer, trying to create

business opportunities out of thin air, got to the desk of a CIO! Bravo!

Karen, what you and your employer don't realize is that you have done irreparable damage to yourself, your company, its other employees and its investors. Your brand arrived at my desk and captured that precious moment of my attention based on a foundation of trickery and deceit. Your very first move to begin a relationship destroyed the opportunity to ever establish credibility.

If you want me to do business with you, you need me to trust you, your company and your product offering. I have to be willing to take a business and professional risk on your organization to invest in your product for use in my business, where I am accountable for performance and quality.

Karen, your elegantly addressed letter demonstrates everything that I need to know to make a business decision. You have no integrity. You have no ethics. You have been permanently written off; I will never consider doing business with you or your employer. You can also let your CEO know that I'll be sure to share my experiences with you and your company at CIO gatherings, where we enjoy trading insights about vendors.

THE TAKEAWAY

Personal letters only work if there's truly a personal relationship.

Liar, Liar, Pants on Fire

My inbox was recently graced with a well-written cold pitch for a technology product that looked interesting, so I gave it a full read. The following line and its subtle peer pressure will sound all too familiar to most CIOs:

Our current clients include Company A, Company B, Company C, Company D and Company E in your industry.

What the writer didn't realize is that despite my sometimes socially limiting career in IT, I know my CIO counterparts at three of the five companies mentioned.

I forwarded the email to each of them to ask the simple question: "Is this product and vendor worth my time to follow up?" A positive answer would have likely persuaded me to call or email the salesperson and learn more.

Unfortunately, not one of my peers had ever heard of the product or vendor. The salesperson never got that call from me. Worse, my email query poisoned the water for them with my three CIO peers.

Would you sign a contract with somebody who started lying at the first meeting? No trust, no sale. Don't assume that I don't have a network. I do, and I'll check your client list myself.

Your networking can work either for or against you. Either way, you will reap what you sow. It's OK to be a small company or a startup or to conservatively state your client list. Every company was once a startup with a small book of business.

THE TAKEAWAY

When touting your clients, own your reality. State facts, use real client lists, and show your value. This ensures your network works for you, not against you.

Top 10 Mistakes Salespeople Make When Cold Calling

Cold calling is a difficult job. I certainly wouldn't want to do it. As a CIO, I try to choose vendors based on research and/or recommendations. Accepting a vendor meeting based on a random email is kind of like buying from eBay: You never know how it'll work out until it's too late.

If you're still determined to use cold calls or cold emails, check out my personal "Top 10 List" first. Here are the top 10 things to avoid—unless you want the CIO to hit the Delete button.

1. *Don't misspell my name.* Do I really need to tell you that? Apparently, for many of you I do.

2. *Don't try to sell restaurant point-of-sale software to the CIO of a health-care company.* Know what my company does before you contact me.

3. *Don't forget to spend five minutes reviewing your email before you hit Send.* Don't just import the email address you got from a mailing list directly into your mail merge program. Letters addressed to "Dear Mr. Smith, L.J." don't have that personal connection you are trying so hard to make.

4. *Don't request a "read receipt" from me.* It's bad enough that Facebook, Google and the NSA are already tracking me; I don't need salespeople doing the same.

5. *Don't offer me a gift card in return for meeting with you.* First, it's just plain sad that you have to bribe people into meeting with you. Second, accepting gifts from vendors violates most company policies (and maybe even some laws). Finally, it's insulting that you think I'm desperate enough to give up my valuable time or forgo my ethics for a Starbucks gift card.

6. *Don't have your assistant invite me to a meeting.* Any email that starts out, "My Director, Mr. X, is in your area on Tuesday April 22 at 9:15 and would like to meet with you" gets deleted, pronto. (Better yet, I'll have my assistant delete it.)

7. *Don't send an email the instant after you leave a voice-mail.* If I had had the time or inclination to answer the phone when you called, I would have.

8. *Don't be afraid to give up.* Persistence may be a virtue, but there is a limit. When you receive no reply after three attempts to contact me, don't keep filling my email and voicemail inboxes with additional messages. If I wasn't interested the first five times, I won't be interested the sixth.

9. *Don't send me a list of 10 dates and times you're available to meet with me.* If anything will convince me to meet you, it is a reasoned outline of the product you sell and why it benefits my company, not the fact that you happen to have a few hours free.

10. *Don't solicit me if my company is already a customer.* If we already buy your product or service, we probably won't buy it twice.

Put yourself in my shoes for a moment. I receive 30 or so emails and voicemails per day from well-meaning vendors. If I take even five minutes to understand and adequately respond to each one, I will spend 150 minutes per day, or 12.5 hours per week, on work that has little likelihood of material benefit.

THE TAKEAWAY

Do your research on who I am and what my company does before you cold call me. If you demonstrate what's in it for me, you'll get results.

Are You a Frog or a Good Relational Seller?

We kiss a lot of frogs as CIOs. (I'm sure salespeople kiss their share, too.) Every now and then one of those frogs does their job right and turns out to be an effective relational salesperson. Here's an example:

Dear Mr. CIO,

We have a mutual friend, Jim BestGuyInTheWorld, and he sends his regards.

Jim and I have worked together for many years, and he thought it would be a good idea to reach out to you regarding <project/service that you've worked with Jim on before> and see if I could provide any assistance.

Please let me know if you are available to get together to discuss this, and I would like to offer my assistance if applicable.

Sincerely,

Has-a-Clue-How-to-Build-Relationships

Clue did a great job here. Let's take it point by point:

- Clue found a contact in common, Jim.
- Clue checked in with Jim so that they could reference his referral.
- Clue was sure to mention that Jim wasn't just a one-night-stand contact; Clue has worked with Jim for years, and the relationship is solid.
- Clue suggested value he could offer and invited a discussion.

A clean play. No fouls. Nicely done! And more than that, Clue secured a meeting!

I look forward to having breakfast with Clue and Jim. Yes, Clue is bringing Jim along. Nice move to parlay Clue's relationship on top of my existing relationship with Jim and build from there. Clue is knocking it out of the park before the game even starts.

I don't know what this meeting will lead to, but I'm looking forward to seeing my old friend Jim and getting to know Clue.

THE TAKEAWAY

Don't be a frog. Try building relationships (and building on your relationships) instead.

THE BUDDY SYSTEM

Trying to make a connection with a CIO? Use your existing customer network to help you get into their circle. You have a lot more credibility when someone else is telling your story than when you're telling it yourself.

It's So Easy

Based upon conversations with salespeople, your days are crammed with trying to get meetings while you'd prefer them to be full of great meetings with decision makers.

On the CIO side of the desk, our days are crammed with serving our internal customers, supporting our staffs and advancing our mission. We don't have time that's sitting there just waiting for a meeting.

Competition for our time is tough. Salespeople already know this, but in the drudgery of trying to get meetings, sometimes I think they forget it.

Humans love to complain, and this book contains a fair share of complaints. So, instead of talking about what doesn't work, here's an example of what *does* work. And it's so simple. Walk with me.

- Approach, ask for a meeting, then follow up as the CIO suggests.
- Make it easy for the CIO to meet with you (but don't be a stalker):

    You: I live/work/pick up my kids/shop near your office and can meet at your convenience.

- Agree to suggestions:

    Me: How about breakfast close to my office?
    You: Of course!

- When you meet, make it an interesting conversation. Find and discuss common interests. Establish your credibility with confidence, not swagger.
- Let the conversation run. You'd be surprised what you find out. You may find out who your prospect deals with, why, and how they explore new relationships...without even asking!
- On the way out of the meeting, inquire about follow-up

and accept what you're offered.

- Follow up as the CIO suggests and wait. When a need arises, your credibility, your coolness, and the relationship you've seeded will bear fruit.

I can tell you first-hand that this works for others. It will work for you, too. Not with every prospect, but with more than you expect!

Isn't that easy?

THE TAKEAWAY

The simple process above works for others, and it will work for you. Not with every prospect, but with more than you expect. Sometimes keeping it simple is the best approach.

CHAPTER 2

Do Your Homework

IF YOU THOUGHT THE NEED TO DO HOMEWORK ended when you got out of school, think again. There's no longer any excuse for not learning as much as you can about a prospect before you speak to them. The internet, social media, networking organizations, and your own colleagues and customers are all great resources for unearthing valuable information about the CIOs you want to sell to.

CIOs we spoke to for this book are unanimous on one point: They don't take cold calls or respond to cold emails. Warm them up by learning about their company, their industry, their challenges, their needs and what makes them tick before you ever try to make contact. If you fail to prepare, you're preparing to fail—so keep reading to get ready for success.

Get Smart

I have come to the point that I only answer internal calls. Yes, these are calls from inside my company. I can't take another external call. Why? Because it's usually somebody trying to sell me something I don't want to buy.

Instead, I let the external call go to voicemail, hoping and praying it's not a call from a critical customer or contact that I really should answer.

Yes, salesperson, I have customers, too—but how do I answer their calls when I'm afraid that picking up the phone means talking to yet another salesperson about something I'm probably not going to buy?

On rare occasions I do listen to a voicemail—but only when somebody leaves an "intelligent voicemail."

What's intelligence? Knowing your customer. Follow these three steps to demonstrate intelligence:

1. *Know the company.* There is so much information available in the public domain and online on so many companies, but still it's rare to see a salesperson take the time to do some simple research. I recently read a three-page report from a securities analyst about our company. I was shocked at how much the analyst knew about our business, our goals, and our future direction. In just three pages, he captured the essence of the business—even though he never spoke to anybody from our company. That same information is available to you online. Yes, you, too, can be a smarty pants.

2. *Know what an IT organization looks like.* Should you get the organization chart? Sure, if you can. They're always helpful but not necessary. That's because, while organization charts may differ by company and have more or fewer people in each role, IT organizations are very similar

across industries. It boils down to three things: People can work in multiple areas of IT, but they are either *planning*, *building*, or *running* IT-related stuff for the business. Before you leave your next voicemail or email, know which of these three areas the IT person's role falls into. Here's a closer look at the three areas.

- PLAN people are creating roadmaps for the future of IT, with a focus on the business. They are enterprise architects, senior IT leaders, and senior business analysts. They're powerful people if you can get to them because they usually know what's important to the business and what IT has to do to fulfill the business's plans.

  PLAN people often have limited budgets. They are strategic thinkers but are already planning for next year and probably not helpful for spending this year. Catch them in Q3 or Q4 when they have influence on budget. Five to 10% of the IT budget for a company is typically for PLAN.

- BUILD people handle projects that provide value to the business. They get their direction from the planners. BUILD people usually have budget to spend, and they need help getting their projects done for the business. They are program managers, technical architects, and business analysts. Start by selling to the technical architects and business analysts, then move up to the program managers.

  Once the build is done, the BUILD people give their project to the RUN people. Remember, BUILD is only 10% of the life cycle of a project; 90% of the remaining life cycle cost goes to RUN. If you're lucky, 20% to 30% of a company's IT budget is in BUILD.

- RUN people are running day-to-day operations for

both infrastructure and applications support. Much of RUN is outsourced these days, and it's hard to get sales traction here because it is so commoditized. IT organizations are moving aggressively to the cloud and abandoning their data centers. At my company, we're redeploying our day-to-day internal RUN people and using managed services from large or boutique providers for infrastructure and applications support. This is a commodity-based business that is cost sensitive, so cost savings with quality is ultimately what matters.

The RUN people may not be doing the work, but they are often leading and managing the cloud providers or outsourcers. If you're lucky, 60% to 80% of the company's budget is in RUN. For many IT organizations, particularly older companies with lots of legacy systems, RUN can easily be 85% to 95% of the IT budget.

3. *Know what's important to the CIO.* IT organizations sometimes think they're unique, but usually they're not. While the priorities for the CIO vary by business and by industry, many of the "Top 10 IT Priorities" continue to be the same year over year (e.g., business intelligence). Others on the list are newcomers (e.g., digital transformation.). If you're speaking to a CIO, you should know and understand the Top 10 Priorities for IT regardless of business or industry. If that's what matters to the CIO, sell based on the Top 10. (You can grab lists like this from Gartner and many other analysts.)

THE TAKEAWAY

Before you leave your next voicemail or email, do some homework, and get to know me and my business. Invest your time if you want mine.

What's In It for Me?

Every week I get the same wonderful offer from vendors:
an opportunity to learn. This week, like every other week,
I had a dozen or so vendors leave me these generous messages. Some leave them on voicemail, some leave them on
email, and 90% of them leave a message in both places, with
a second message letting me know that you left me a message
in the first place.

Every one of these offers goes like this:

*We would like to come out to hear about what initiatives
you have going on, learn about what you are working
on and what your top priorities are, and figure out how
we can help you.*

Oh, I see: This is a learning opportunity *for the vendor*!

You want me to take my time to inform you about our company so you can tell me how you can solve all my problems.

If I agreed to all these offers, meeting with vendors is all
I would ever do.

I ignore all these requests. The only informational ses-
sions I'll ever consider come as direct referrals from people
I know and respect.

It's not my job to inform you. Do your homework to learn
about a company's initiatives and priorities before you pitch
the CIO in the first place.

THE TAKEAWAY

Don't ask the CIO to give up valuable time to educate you;
educate yourself.

Learn My Language

I'm more sympathetic to salespeople than some of my counterparts because I have worked in sales. I've been on the other side, from a hardware, software, reseller and services perspective. I know how hard it is, and I've made some mistakes.

But I also know how easily you can build street credibility by taking a few basic steps. One of these is learning the CIO's language.

There's very little that's effective in a cold email or cold call, period. But in a warm email, warm call or first meeting, what *is* effective is someone who has done everything they can to understand what business we're in, and what challenges and projects we have going on.

If you're pitching me, this involves looking at my LinkedIn feed, looking at the company LinkedIn feed, doing a Google search on a couple of terms, looking at the vendors I might mention and seeing who won business.

That's literally 20 minutes' worth of research. Doing that before you come in the office goes a long way, because it shows you're trying to use my language.

It's the same as when you travel internationally. When you visit most countries, if the locals know you're trying to speak their language, they'll be sympathetic and will try to help you in any way possible. I operate the same way, and our team operates the same way.

From a sales perspective, if you're trying to speak our language, you've taken the time to learn a little bit about what we're doing, so we're going to open up to you much more readily than to someone who walks in and clearly knows nothing about us.

Even if they know our industry well, if they know nothing

about us, they lose street credibility.

Before trying to pitch a CIO and start a relationship, why not take a few minutes to learn about the company you hope to sell to?

THE TAKEAWAY

Speaking a common language eases the road to the sale. Taking the time to learn about the CIO and the company adds credibility to your cause.

DO YOU HAVE A HAMMER?

There's not always a fit between the CIO's need and the salesperson's solution. Too many salespeople don't comprehend that that is even possible. If you've got a hammer to sell, my problem must look like a nail, right? If you want to find the fit, do your homework to find a meaningful connection between what the prospect does, their business challenges, and your solutions.

What Do They Really Do All Day?

Do you know what a CIO does?

Most of what a CIO does is not about technology or software.

- It's about having strong business acumen to contribute to the organization's strategy and innovation conversations.
- It's about being an agent for competitive differentiation and enterprise transformation.
- It's about providing leadership to all the people who support IT, regardless of the logo on their badges.
- It's about building and maintaining relationships with internal and external stakeholders (e.g., regulators, partners, and yes, even vendors).
- It's about efficient and cost-effective use of the organization's resources.
- It's about revenue-generating products and services.
- It's about safeguarding the organization's reputation through best-in-class management of security, privacy, and compliance activities.
- In summary, the role of the CIO is about partnership to achieve enterprise-wide success. Please think about how you can contribute to that the next time you call on me.

THE TAKEAWAY

Understand the CIO's role and how you can contribute to it before you approach them.

Understanding the CIO's Agenda

CIOs have an agenda. Salespeople do, too.

Unfortunately, the two agendas are not the same.

As a senior leader, every CIO has a strategic agenda that's driven by the CEO. If you're selling the latest, greatest storage, and their agenda isn't about the latest, greatest storage, you're wasting your time. You're not going to be successful in selling to the CIO unless it wraps around their agenda.

How do you do that? I worked with one successful salesperson whose products we already used. He wanted to sell us more, so he frequently asked questions to understand our issues, our plans and our problems.

Then he would go off and do his work to understand how his suite of products and services were able to map against our needs. And then he would present them that way. Not all at once, but bit by bit. Every time we met, he'd have one or two ideas to exchange. That's a much better way of selling, and it worked.

Warning: Don't try this tactic with a CIO unless you have an established business relationship. Half the calls I get are from salespeople asking if I have 15 minutes to tell them about our company's issues, plans and problems. I don't have the time or inclination to educate every salesperson on the planet about my needs, but I *do* have time to discuss them with salespeople I already work with.

Companies go through cycles. Sometimes there are cycles when companies are interested in cutting costs. If your product can be positioned to save money, that's a great way to make the sale. But there are all kinds of cycles. You have to figure out the cycle and how your product or service fits into what that company is interested in at that time.

How do you learn that? Do your research before you walk

in to a client meeting or get on a call. Read the company's history and an overview of the financials. Read press articles, analyst reports, whatever you can find on the internet. That gives you a flavor for what the company's challenges are before you ever walk in the door.

Do your homework on the CIO, too. Maybe they've spoken at conferences, published blogs or been interviewed in publications. Find that stuff and read it to get an idea of the CIO's mindset and what they're working on. It helps you position yourself more appropriately.

Today, a salesperson isn't only selling. They're also doing a lot of coordinating and may be leading the charge for providing the analysis that helps support what they're selling. Your job as a salesperson is to make the CIO successful. Whether your product is strategic or transformative, cuts costs or whatever it does, help them make the business case that supports the purchase.

THE TAKEAWAY

Every CIO has their own agenda. Your agenda should be to support theirs.

The Big Switch

Getting a CIO to switch vendors is one of the biggest challenges a salesperson can take on. Unless they're at startups, most CIOs don't need to go searching for vendors—they already have vendors they're happy with (or at least not *unhappy* with).

If you know a CIO is unhappy with a vendor, that's an easy opportunity. But getting my attention and luring me away from a trusted vendor is anything but.

How can you get a CIO to consider you as a replacement for a trusted vendor?

- *Use your connections.* The best way for me to consider switching to a new vendor is if I know a trusted colleague in another firm is already using that vendor with great success. CIOs talk. We ask, "Has anybody heard of this vendor? Are you using them? How do you like them?" Ask yourself which clients you have that your prospect may know, too. How can you connect to a prospect through other people in your industry?

- *Don't bash your competition.* Some vendors try to tell me all the terrible things the incumbent vendor is doing. That's not the way to win my business. Instead, focus on productivity, profits, and how your product or service can impact the core values that are most important to my firm. If you know what's important to me, that should be easy for you to do. Even a 10-minute conversation can have enough impact to make me start wondering, "Should I be looking at another vendor?"

   Here's an example. At my firm, document management software is one of our core applications. There isn't a lot of choice out there—just a few vendors whose products all do basically the same thing. But it's my practice to regularly reach out to new vendors to see what they have in development. When I did that with an opposing vendor and brought them in for a meeting, they didn't try to talk me out of our current software. Instead, they did a great job of explaining why I *should* be using *their* product and what differentiated it. They knew what my needs were and did a very targeted presentation.

- *Don't push.* After that meeting, there was zero pressure to sign a deal. The vendor gave me the time to process the information. They came in 10 more times over the next year, doing the same presentation for different stakeholder groups. They never said, "Do we really have to do this again?" They were always happy to come in, do the presentation and answer any questions that came up.

- *Know the audience.* Throughout all these meetings, the vendor honed their presentation based on who was in each meeting. From a document management perspective, the conversation you have with the end user vs. the IT person is a very different conversation. IT can't make the buying decision alone; there are others who need to be persuaded. This vendor always brought in the right people for the audience—people who could speak the right "language," whether it was lawyers for a meeting with attorneys, or IT people for a meeting with the IT team.

- *Educate the prospect.* While all of this was going on, they regularly invited me to events they were holding so I could learn more about their product. They had a depth of knowledge and were always able to get us to the people we needed to answer our questions.

- *Be professional.* When we finally decided to sign a deal and move to the new document management system, the new vendor was extremely professional and collegial with the old vendor. They worked with the other vendor and were willing to do whatever it took to make sure that the transition went smoothly. They put a lot of effort into it before they even got a dime.

THE TAKEAWAY

With patience, persistence and targeted persuasion, you can woo a client away from an existing vendor—even if they're currently satisfied.

IT'S NOT YOU, IT'S ME

Salespeople love to talk about their product and their service. I'll tell you a secret: I don't really care about your product or service. What I care about is whether you know me and my company and how your product or service relates to me or my business.

It's the Little Things

Salespeople try a lot of tricks to get your attention. I'm not into tricks. What gets my attention is when somebody has done their research. If you're really interested in meeting with me and feel that you could have an impact on my firm, do your homework.

For example, I had a vendor that had been calling and emailing me, and I hadn't had a chance to get back to him. Then I got a Villanova University mug in the mail (I went to Villanova). That made an impression—not because I want to get gifts or need vendors to spend money on me, but because he did his research. Later, Villanova was in March Madness finals and he sent me an email about that. Soon we were talking, because he connected with me through something that was meaningful to me.

Another vendor kept calling me every day at three o'clock in the afternoon. I was never in my office. Finally, one day I answered the phone. I was pregnant at the time and jokingly said, "I'm pregnant; I go out at three o'clock every day for ice cream." The next thing I know, I got an ice cream scoop and set of ice cream bowls in the mail from the salesperson.

Things like that don't make me want to buy a vendor's product, but they do create a personal connection. Of course, not all CIOs like getting gifts, so part of doing your homework is learning how the CIO feels about gifts. Do they love or hate them? Does their company have a policy against accepting gifts? Some CIOs need a "warm" connection to accept gifts from salespeople; others don't mind receiving gifts from salespeople they don't know. The CIO's administrative assistant is the best person to ask about this. They can also advise you of the CIO's travel schedule, so you avoid mistakes like the time a salesperson sent me a cake with the Magic

Quadrant on it. I was on vacation, and the cake emulsified while I was gone. (I'm just glad it didn't attract ants!)

On a company level, a salesperson might send me an email referencing that our office is in Philadelphia and say they have connections there they can leverage for us. I'm also impressed when a vendor comes in to do a presentation and they know exactly where all our offices are so they can say things like, "Your people in Denver will do X, and your people in DC will do Y."

Vendors who don't pay attention to the details might mention our Houston office. Well, we don't have a Houston office.

That's a little thing, but it shows they pay attention and have taken the time to learn about your business. When you have limited time, as all CIOs do, you want a salesperson you can make a connection with and move fast without having to educate them about what you do.

THE TAKEAWAY

When you're trying to connect with a CIO, the little things make a big difference.

Get the G2 on the CIO

Getting to a CIO in a traditional way just doesn't happen anymore. Picking up the phone, sending email, connecting on LinkedIn or trying to outwit the admin works about 1% of the time these days.

Frustration with this can drive salespeople to do some crazy things. I spoke to hundreds of sales reps for this book, and you wouldn't believe some of the stories I heard.

One rep hired a private investigator to follow the CIO and find out where they went to dinner, played golf and vacationed, just so the rep could "bump into" them one day. Yes, salespeople have a tough job, but that's over the top.

Making connections is a journey. If your company doesn't have the patience to let you marinate for a bit and build a brand, get the hell out of there. Find a place that appreciates the hunt—those companies are out there. Don't be the salesperson who hops around to five jobs in four years. First, it's exhausting; second, explaining why you did that gets old fast.

Find a home, build your brand and wonderful things will come your way. To get the G2 on your target and their needs— and make connections the right way—try these tips.

- *Get social.* I follow my network on Twitter and Facebook. This gives me great information about their business and personal interests and even their birthdays. I always send a personal message wishing them a happy birthday. It's a little thing, but people appreciate it, and it can differentiate you from the other folks.
- *Make it an event.* Your CIO network travels to many conferences and awards ceremonies. Get your company to buy a booth, sponsor something or let you attend. These events are a great way to make connections with CIOs. They'll feel obligated to give you face time, and as long

as you create a meaningful dialog, it opens the door a crack for you to follow up.

- *Get referrals.* The #1 way to connect is via referral. The network is king. Ask your connections to make a soft introduction. If they respect you and your company and value you, they'll do it.
- *Help them connect.* Connecting the CIOs in your network to each other is a great way to build credibility. Many CIOs, especially those who are new to the area, want to meet their peers. This is a great way to build your personal brand without trying to sell something. No one likes to be sold—so don't do it until the time is right.
- *Give back.* Make a connection outside the work environment. Find out what boards, charitable organizations and local service clubs CIOs are involved in. I've spent eight years on the board of a local organization that helps underserved 18-to-25-year-olds find their way. I teach a life skills class for this group.

I originally got involved to make connections, because the organization is peppered with local IT leadership. I don't take advantage of this, but I use the connections wisely and have gained tremendous access to CIOs as a result.

But I've also gained something more. What started as a selfish act to gain access to CIOs turned into an obsession to help the organization's clients better themselves and find a place in the world. Find a cause and it will help you in all sorts of ways.

—*The Super Salesperson*

THE TAKEAWAY

Connecting with CIOs can't be rushed. Take time to approach CIOs like you would anyone else, and you'll make connections that pay off.

ANALYZE THIS

Looking for more information on a prospect's company? Securities analysts are smart, well-compensated people. They are paid for their ability to quickly express the essence of a company to potential investors. They've done the research for you, so steal it from them.

The Dual Role CIO

I lead both marketing and IT for my company. Most sales-people in both arenas don't realize that strange combination can exist.

Depending on which "hat" salespeople think they are calling, I get very different approaches. Sometimes two reps from the same vendor call me separately, one for each persona.

When salespeople think they are calling the head of marketing, I usually hear:

- Babble designed to treat me as though I am technophobic and technically impaired
- Ideas for how I can cut the IT department mercilessly out of my life
- How bad our website and mobile strategy is because of "those tech guys"
- How I'd better jump on the cloud, mobile, social media, and analytics trains before I am out of business

When salespeople think they are calling the head of IT, I usually hear:

- Marketing jargon designed to treat me as though I am creatively inept and business-impaired
- How I can make the marketing department like me and not cut me out of the company
- How bad our website and mobile strategy is because of "those marketing guys"
- How I'd better jump on the cloud, mobile, social media, and analytics trains before I am out of business

The common talking points seem to boil down to:

- Prospects are impaired and should be treated as such.
- Playing business functions against each other is a winning sales strategy.
- Insulting the prospect's product or work will inspire

an embarrassed rush to sign a contract.

- Prospects (being impaired) are too backward to have considered (much less rejected) all the current IT trends.
- IT and Marketing can't possibly talk to each other, much less have a common executive managing them.

When people find out I hold both jobs, there is an audible squeal of brakes as tongues and minds come screeching to a halt.

The modern CIO and CMO are increasingly connected and frequently are even the same person. It's time for your sales approach to acknowledge and embrace this.

When selling to either the CIO or CMO (or really, to anyone):

- Treat us like we are smart and capable adults who have a need you might be able to fill.
- Treat us like we work as part of a common team that wants to succeed (not as enemies that want to tear each other down).
- Deliver proof of how great you are at providing that web/mobile/other service (not criticism of how badly we are doing it).
- Understand that our job is to run a business (not to jump on the latest fad or trend).

Find out what we know, then educate us if needed. Don't babble, insult or divide. Treat us like adults instead of the infighting kids you sometimes make us out to be.

THE TAKEAWAY

Traditional divisions between IT and other business divisions are breaking down. Assume that CIOs share information and may even share roles with other C-level executives.

How can a salesperson make a good impression?

"They said, 'Look, I've done research on your company, and I don't think our product works for you right now. But here is where I think you may be going, and you may need us later. I'd like to start talking to you now because my research says in a year or so you may need a product like ours, and I'd like to stay in touch.'"

"I was moving to a new state. A salesperson learned from a mutual friend that I was a foodie, so as a welcome gift, she sent me an index card beautifully written in calligraphy with the best restaurants, wine shops and cheese shops she recommended in the area."

"By showing me that their product has helped somebody who has similar challenges and somebody who has credibility with me."

"Be prepared, be patient and be available. I often tell salespeople sometimes you just have to be around to be top of mind and be considered when the need arises."

Get Attention the Right Way

At the risk of giving away the secret of someone who knows how to do it right, I offer the following email as an example of a sales pitch gone well. How refreshing! I wish more people would go about it like this person did.

Hello <insert the target's name>

Congratulations on your recent <insert successes or publicly visible things about the company>. It's great to see a local company doing so well and moving their industry forward.

I was researching <insert company name> because I am impressed by your <insert what impresses you>. I see that you have an open position for <insert title> with some very exciting projects envisioned for this role.

At <your company's name>, I help people like you who are rolling out these types of projects and can support your in-house efforts through <name your value-added services>. We work with you in whatever way is most effective for you, from providing light consulting through full implementation support.

Would you be interested in speaking with me about this or any other areas where you are looking for support and how I might be able to help you?

Sincerely, <insert your name>

This approach shows me:

- You did your homework.
- You identify with my company as a company and not just as the next prospect on your list.
- You want to add value.
- You didn't obnoxiously suggest you are the one I need; instead, you asked to talk more.
- You said you "might" be able to add value, rather than

arrogantly state you are "sure you can."

In short, you invited a discussion starting at the highest level—about my company, products, market results and culture—and are willing to work from there. You *did not* ask me what projects I have that you can help me with. You proved you already did your research, so you had a place to start.

This approach can't be pulled out on a moment's notice and applied in any situation. You need to time it around something positive happening at my company. You'll know when you can use it because you've been watching my company over time, following the news, and making connections.

In short, this approach requires attention over time—the same kind of attention I expect once I'm a customer. Show me that attention as a prospect, and there's a much better chance I'll become a customer.

This person got an immediate email back, got a lunch meeting within the month, and got recommended to members of my team as well as others outside my company as someone to check out and engage with.

Wouldn't you love to be this person?

THE TAKEAWAY

Give me your attention when I'm a prospect, and you have a much better chance of turning me into a customer.

CHAPTER 3

Building Relationships

IF YOU EXPECT YOUR INITIAL CONTACT WITH A CIO to lead directly to a sale, slow down. Why settle for one quick sale when, with a little patience, you can have so much more? Instead of striving for a signature on a contract, make it your goal to build lasting relationships with the CIOs you serve.

How do you build relationships? Hint: You don't do it through email blasts, social media or constant phone calls. In this chapter, we share the do's and don'ts of building lasting relationships with CIOs—even those who don't need what you're selling right now.

LinkedIn Is Not a Dating Service

Working hard today? Sitting around the house or office, trolling the LinkedIn listings, using some advanced search feature that you or your company paid LinkedIn for? Checking out people on the "People You May Know" screen? Somehow, my profile pops up. BAM. You're a winner!

Now you do the real hard work of clicking that "Connect" button. You don't even take the time to add a personalized note (yes, you can do that!). You did your job for the day and are probably tossing back a brew or sipping a fine glass of wine. I mean, wow, you just snagged an invite to a real CIO!

I'm working hard too. I'm dealing with delivering value to customers. I'm fighting the daily battle of high uptime, low-cost, unclear requirements and demands to deliver. I'm working my tail off. Instead of a brew or a glass of wine, what I got to end my day was a LinkedIn connection request from someone I don't know (that's you!). Cheap date. Go away. I click the "X," not the check mark. You're done.

See, I'm an old-fashioned guy. Being "in my network" means, well, you're "in my *network*." I know you. Knowing you means that I have met you in person or had a business relationship with you. Sometimes I'll accept a LinkedIn request from a friend of a friend—if my friend has vouched for you already. But for over 90% of my LinkedIn connections, I have met you, I know you, and could introduce you to someone else in a meaningful way. That's what being in my network means.

I don't collect connections. I build them through networking, meeting people, doing business, and sharing common interests. Don't you want to be in *that* group, and not just some cheap, drive-by connection request?

I have an idea. It's a novel concept, but please follow along. How about you use that LinkedIn tool as it was intended to be used? Find someone who knows me, knows you and can vouch for you. Then ask them to introduce us!

There are, after all, over 500 people in my network, and if one of them recommends you, I'm bound to engage in a discussion with you.

After that, you just might end up "in my network," which means I'd know you, do business with you and vouch for you. After all, that's what you want, isn't it? Not a cheap date, but a meaningful business relationship that meets both of our needs. Right?

THE TAKEAWAY

Use LinkedIn as a tool for connecting with people you really have links to—not as an online dating service.

DROP THE NAME-DROPPING

Salespeople who name-drop and offer to share information about what my competitors are doing is a pet peeve. If you're going to share confidential information about another client with me, are you sharing my confidential information with them too? Respect your clients, respect me, and don't reveal inside information.

Salesperson or Stalker: What's the Difference?

Real stalking is a crime. In sales, it rarely pays off. One January, a few years back, I received two stalking attacks within two weeks of the ball dropping in Time Square:

Hi Mr. CIO, I just dropped you an email, and I listened to your voice mail greeting, and I am going to reach out to your assistant as you advised, but I just wanted to let you know that I am John from Helpful Consultants Inc., and we have high-caliber consultants ready to go.

Is John getting a call or email back? Doubtful! One of my New Year's resolutions was to reduce clutter. In less than one minute I deleted the voice mail and the email, and I told my assistant to ignore him. Clutter gone!

Hi Mr. CIO, you may have missed my last email, so I'm sending you this reminder to pop it back to the top of your inbox. At Ship Your Gizmo, we have a full stock of IT equipment that we can get out to you today! All I need is 10 minutes on your busy calendar so that we can discuss your needs.

Truth be told, Ship had sent me at least five emails, one every few days. I don't need Ship to manage my inbox—I'm good at it. I see Ship's name, and I hit the Delete button. Bye-bye.

John from Helpful is certainly not being helpful. Neither is Ship. Both are stalkers, pure and simple. I don't know if the fault is theirs, their employers', or both.

Of course, if your boss rates you by the number of calls made or the number of emails sent, you'll pummel my peers and me with these worthless approaches. As a wear-em-down salesperson, these tactics might land you a sale here and there, but they won't build relationships. This approach is annoying to the target and mostly unproductive to the stalker.

Meaningful interactions lead to enduring business

relationships. You get those interactions and relationships by networking your way to influential people.

Just think about it...when you need something, who do you call? Someone you know and like, not someone who bugs you.

THE TAKEAWAY

If you are a stalker, do the work to become a real salesperson. If your employer is forcing you to stalk, find a new employer who values business relationships and allows you to take the time to build them.

TAKE IT OUTSIDE

Getting the CIO out of the office whenever possible is a great way to build relationships. Find a fun activity that gives you time to relax, chat and share a laugh or two. Golf is the traditional option, but think outside the green too. What about wine tasting, skeet shooting, hiking, hot air balloon rides, or a day of deep-sea fishing? Sharing an experience creates memories and bonds. (Do your homework first, of course. Otherwise you might invite a member of PETA to go quail hunting and make the wrong kind of impression.)

Are You a Bad Blind Date?

What I call "the contact trifecta" is an amazing and annoying thing. It's amazing that the technology exists for a "suitor" (read salesperson) to do all the following at almost the exact same time:

1. Cold call and leave me a meaningless "please call me back" voice mail.
2. Email me with the same useless, usually scripted content that was already included in the voice mail.
3. Send me a request to connect on LinkedIn.

Frequently, all three of these contact methods come in within seconds. That doesn't mean they work.

This three-pronged approach fails because:

I need a value proposition and a worthwhile action to take. I rarely have time or interest to idly chat. I haven't had it since I was a dating teenager, and you don't remind me of the first girl I ever kissed. If I gave 10 to 15 minutes to everyone who asked for it, I would spend all day on useless calls.

My email and voice mail both function fine. The approach of leaving a voice mail "to see if you got my email" or vice versa may seem coy to you. At best, it is offensive to my tech team, who ensures those messages get delivered more than 99.999% of the time. If I wasn't already ignoring you, insulting our infrastructure would ensure I do it.

A good CIO is a connector who brokers relationships. LinkedIn is my Rolodex and my networking currency. After the above two incursions, do you really think I want to foist you upon my LinkedIn friends like some bad blind date?

Would you trust a potential partner who stalked you using multiple mediums and insulted the people you like?

Relationships are built on trust, time and mutual action. As a starting point, let's try sharing thought leadership, leaving actionable messages and providing useful information. Once we trust each other, then we can move on to the transactional stuff . . . and maybe eventually, we can even be LinkedIn friends.

THE TAKEAWAY

A relationship rarely gets better than the first impression. Don't blow it by being desperately aggressive right off the bat.

EMPLOYERS DON'T LAST; RELATIONSHIPS DO

One vendor we were working with was doing such a bad job with implementation, there was talk of suing them. Then they switched out their account team. The new salesperson offered to do whatever it took to get implementation back on track. He was willing to sign a three-year contract and provide resources at cost for that time. They would make no money on the deal, but they weren't there to earn money; they were there to earn our trust, which they had lost. Ten years later, I'm still connected with that individual. When you build a relationship with a CIO, you've got something that can outlast your employment or their employment.

Why Can't We Be Friends?

Vendor, supplier or partner? How do you think about the people and companies that support your IT organization?

Choose your favorite dictionary or thesaurus, and here are some of the descriptions you'll find:

- *Vendor*: seller, hawker, peddler, dealer, merchant
- *Supplier*: contractor, dealer, trader, broker, purveyor
- *Partner*: spouse, companion, colleague, collaborator, lover

I think all CIOs would agree that we need *partners* to accomplish the complex work we are asked to do. Long gone are the days when our internal IT team could do all the work.

These partners may come from different companies that have sales and service goals, but the best IT firms I have worked with don't dwell on those expectations when we are together. They spend their time thinking about how they can make my company more successful.

I'm not looking for a lover, but a collaborator and trusted colleague would sure be nice.

Since this relationship needs to work for both parties, I asked a few of my "partners" what they look for in a great CIO. Here's some of what I heard:

- Take time to help salespeople understand what we need help with.
- Be direct and honest with salespeople.
- Treat salespeople with respect.
- Show up for scheduled meetings and be present.

I next asked a few fellow CIOs what they look for in a great partner. Many of the themes overlapped. The CIO group wants salespeople to:

- Respect the CIO's time.
- Be honest with their offering.

- Bring use cases and industry best practices to the conversation.
- Tell the CIO when you can help but also when you can't. Admitting you don't have the solution a prospect needs goes a long way in building trust.

THE TAKEAWAY

Strive to be a partner, not just a vendor or supplier.

KNOW YOUR CUSTOMER

Some CIOs are captivated by capabilities and the latest bells and whistles. Others are focused more on the true cost of ownership. Knowing your audience is important. Not everyone is sold by the same message, and the things that turn me off might be the exact things that turn someone else on. Learn what works for each person and what doesn't, then tailor your message to that person.

When Is a CIO Not a CIO?

Organizations offering IT services seem to be taking a new approach that's making the role of sales harder for sales professionals and prospects alike. Here's an example:

I recently received two separate LinkedIn invitations from CIO-level individuals. When an invite comes from a peer, I typically look at it and connect if we have some shared connections and nothing else seems odd.

I enjoy having the opportunity to network and learn from my fellow IT leaders. There's a lot to be gained from connecting with other CIOs. For example, recently my organization was replacing a legacy solution and were considering a few alternatives to the incumbent. I reached out to a colleague in San Francisco whose company was mentioned in a press release as having selected one of the vendors we were considering. She arranged to connect my team with the people at her firm that led the selection and contracting process. They gave us their perspective on the vendor and answered our questions.

Getting this type of reference is a great way to supplement to the vendor's officially supplied references. That's because official vendor references typically have some form of an incentive plan in place with the vendor. They earn points or credits in return for serving as a reference.

Back to the LinkedIn invitations: Both were from CIOs of IT services organizations. I took the risk of connecting, and immediately their true MO emerged. These people weren't CIOs looking to connect with their peers for the value of learning from each other. They were looking to connect for targeted business development. Each followed up with a sales pitch for their company and asked to speak with me on the CIO-to-CIO level.

Each of these CIOs turned out to be a CIO in name only. This new trend is exploitative, underhanded, and muddies the waters for all of us. If we can't trust other CIOs, who can we trust?

THE TAKEAWAY
Don't use your CIO as a business development tool.

What's the strangest way a salesperson has tried to build a relationship with you?

"One salesperson always positioned themselves at the same table at the Starbucks where I went every morning, waiting to 'run into' me."

"They invited me to a 'gentleman's club.' I'm a woman."

"I hate sales disguised as consulting. 'Let us help you build a roadmap around what you're doing,' and it turns out the roadmap involves only their solutions."

Are You Running a Marathon or a Sprint?

Recently, I was sitting in the office of a buddy (let's call him Mr. VP) who's an IT leader at a big company in Philadelphia. They have a substantial IT budget and a variety of technology partners.

I noticed him reading an email that seemed to get him pretty disturbed. He immediately picked up the phone and dialed someone we'll call Paul from ABC Software Company. Mr. VP immediately started to read Paul the riot act:

Who do you think you are, going around me to my CIO and telling him I didn't do my job? We have purchased millions of dollars of your software in the past. Pick up the phone and call me directly if you have an issue with the decision. You are done doing business here. Goodbye!

What happened?

Seems Paul had a proposal on the table and Mr. VP and his team had chosen another partner. In desperation, Paul sent an email to the CIO telling him Mr. VP and his team had chosen another partner—and made a mistake that would cost the company money in the long run. Paul also claimed that the playing field wasn't even because he didn't get the access he needed along the way.

All sales veterans have probably been in this situation before. I know I have. You believe you have the better solution, and the customer didn't give you the access and time needed to qualify the proper way and propose the right solution.

I personally can't stand to lose, but sometimes there are newer and better technologies out there that outshine yours. It's hard not to take it personally, but you must understand that this sales gig is a marathon, not a sprint. You will win some and lose some along the way. It's how you handle the situation that prevails in the end.

Rather than sending that email to the CIO (who happens to highly respect Mr. VP), call Mr. VP himself and set up a time to be debriefed about the missed opportunity.

Nine times out of 10, the VP or CIO will respect your request to discuss why they chose another vendor. Most of them will be happy to discuss it with you. You will get the desired face time, build credibility, and stand a better chance of getting the access you need the next time around.

I must admit, I had a smile on my face when Mr. VP was laying into Paul. It was one less vendor I had to compete with, and I knew it would make a great chapter for this book.

—*The Super Salesperson*

THE TAKEAWAY

Never go around your prospect to his or her higher-ups. You'll poison the well for future interactions.

Sell Nothing, Gain Everything

What's my biggest "pain point?" Many days, it's aggressive salespeople.

Let's be serious: We both know you aren't really trying to solve my problem or enable my success. You're trying to make a sale. You clog my inbox, seek to waste my time in increments of "just 15 minutes," and feel the need to call to make sure I got the email I am ignoring.

You have a choice of two paths: the low-return activity of forcefully attempting to close a single sale, or the high-return activity of developing a relationship and expanding your network.

Many of you will choose to pursue the first path and keep chasing the outcome that is less likely to succeed. The results will, unsurprisingly, be less than you desired and more painful than you hoped.

Is the prospect of coercing your way into one possible transaction more exciting and rewarding than the prospect of expanding your network and the possibilities that come with a wider set of connections?

The two paths are simple:

Path 1:

- Establish a relationship.
- Gain my trust.
- Gain access to my network.
- Don't try to "sell" me.
- Expand your audience and influence.

Path 2:

- Sell hard to me.
- Annoy me.
- Lose potential access to my network.
- Get poor reviews when people ask about you.

- Give everyone in my network the same hard sell and get the same results.

You and I both want to do business with people we like and trust. Why not treat me the way you would want to be treated?

Today, try something different. Instead of selling, seek to build relationships, make connections and develop a network. The network will do the work for you by increasing your reputation, your referrals, and ultimately your business.

THE TAKEAWAY

Focus on the relationship, not the transaction.

MAKE YOUR EVENT WORTHWHILE

Trying to attract CIOs to your lunch and learn, event or conference? Savvy CIOs know external learning is as important as internal learning, but they don't have time to spend listening to a low-level person. Bring in an industry or sector leader—a marquee name. I recently went to a lunch and learn with the former heads of the FBI and the Department of Homeland Security. Now, that was high-value-added.

4 Ways to Kill a Relationship

Sales is built on relationships—but relationships are fragile things. Are you making any of the following mistakes? Any one of them can easily kill a relationship.

Mistake 1: Bragging

Even some of our strongest vendors sometimes come into meetings redundantly telling us how awesome they are, I don't care about that. If we invite someone in for a meeting, we've already done the research to know they have value to offer. If you come in initially and try to sell me on the value that I've already established you have, it just smells desperate.

Mistake 2: Relying on the Past

Salespeople who have current knowledge about us or current relationships with us are higher value than those who don't. I periodically get messages from an incredibly persistent service provider who was a rep for a company we did business with seven years ago. He always reminds me that because of his experience with us and how well he knows us, he would be the best provider we could possibly imagine.

I don't care how good this provider is. In a business environment that moves as quickly as today's, how could knowing a little bit about us seven years ago tell him all the changes we've been through over the last six years? He knows nothing about us. The fact that he's persistently saying he does just underscores that he doesn't.

Mistake 3: Buddy-buddy

Some folks get in the door and want to become your buddy right away. They get overly familiar very quickly. They want to do lunch and dinner incessantly. They pepper you with tickets to ball games and concerts.

Thanks, but no thanks. That's a very late-1990s, pre-dot-bomb way of selling. "Let me let me give you some stuff, and you'll give me some business." Almost nobody does business like that anymore, and when a salesperson exhibits behavior in that direction, that's ethical red flags all over the place.

Mistake 4: Funny Business

Some salespeople have no sense of humor. Others have too much of a sense of humor. Both are problems.

Sales folks need to attune themselves to their audience. At my company, we tend to be looser and lighter; it breaks the tension. I appreciate sales teams that understand we're not hyper-formal; they don't need to walk on eggshells.

But sometimes people read that as being hyper-*informal*, and they go a different direction: way too informal. Any initial sales meeting that involves profanity and vulgarity is a bad move. Once you get to know us, you might drop a couple cuss words every now and again—I don't care. But there are folks who come in and drop F-bombs in the first meeting. It's important to be able to read the audience and tune in to the client company's culture.

THE TAKEAWAY

It's easier than you think to kill a relationship before it ever gets off the ground. Proceed with caution and take the client's behavior as your cue.

Happy to Serve

Service impresses me. I don't mean customer service: I mean service to community, industry and others.

Many of my best relationships have started and grown through common involvement in charitable, community and industry organizations. By giving back, I have been introduced to others who are giving back to the world around them.

Giving back is one of the easiest ways to meet me and impress me. Showing you care, over the long term, about something other than yourself reveals your character and commitment. It makes me want to work with you.

Ask yourself what you and your company can do to help those around you. Can you commit to a charity, a volunteer opportunity or a professional group? Should you make an investment of time, money or talent? What can you do selflessly for someone else?

Then go do it—not to "network" but just because it's the right thing to do.

When the time is right, we will intersect at an event or through mutual colleagues. I will know and see what you are doing to help others. It will impress me, and we will have a conversation. Maybe a relationship will grow. Maybe business will come from it.

Either way, you will be doing something good for its own sake, and that is its own reward.

Too many salespeople join organizations only for what they can get out of it. I've been on the board of directors of a technology nonprofit for 12 years. Recently, one individual who was on the advisory board suddenly started showing up at events. He had never attended a single event until then. Turns out he was in a career transition and wanted to make connections.

A lot of folks know how to get into the same network with CIOs, but are you there just trying to make a connection, or are you there doing things for the organization? Are you only going to participate when you have something to gain?

Don't be a fraudster. CIOs can tell.

THE TAKEAWAY

When you take the time to give back to others, you'll reap much more than connections.

KNOW WHEN TO SAY NO

It builds a lot of trust when a salesperson is honest enough to say, "We can help you with X, but actually, our competitor has a better solution for Y." Being a salesperson who doesn't say "Yes, we can do that" all the time creates credibility. If you tell me when you can't do something, the next time you say you can do it, I'll know you really can.

Participation Pays Off

I met the co-author of this book (let's call him Super Salesman) a few years back. I didn't meet Super in a sales role. I met him as a guy at a conference having dinner with friends.

Super was there to casually make contacts with CIOs and those in the tech industry. Sure, he was there to sell, but not right then. He was there to get to know people and enjoy some golf and good Florida weather.

He sponsored a dinner by getting a few friends together and asking them to bring a few friends. I was a friend of a friend. At the time, and throughout dinner, I wasn't sure who was sponsoring the event, but I enjoyed the discussion and the food.

At some point, Super started a discussion about his blog. A month or so later, after we had a relationship established, he started a discussion about his business.

Not only did I become a contributor to his blog, but like the famous commercial says, I also became a customer (and a promoter of his company).

So why don't more people get involved, participate and build real relationships? I don't know!

The alternatives really stink:

- *Alternative No. 1: Cold Calls*
  My telephone rings all day. Nearly every one of those calls is someone cold-calling me to make sure I'm aware of their services, to offer that they are available to contribute to my most important initiatives (that they are dying to learn of), or to suggest that I'd be doing my employer a disservice if I didn't return their call right today. Get real, folks.
- *Alternative No. 2: Spam Email*
  My inbox is overflowing. No, I don't have "10 minutes" to chat with you. When I delete all the cold-call emails,

I'm down to just a few meaningful emails each day. Busy executives must focus their time and energy. Stop wasting ours.

There is a mutually supportive alternative:

Plenty of opportunities abound for those in the vendor community to get involved in the tech community, support it and build real relationships. The money spent on the constant barrage of phone calls and emails can be redirected toward meaningful industry participation.

That means getting out and doing things, contributing, meeting people and building relationships. Sponsoring an event, buying a table at a fund-raiser, speaking at an event to share your insights, creating a peer networking opportunity (that doesn't require someone to sit through a sales pitch), connecting acquaintances and friends over a casual dinner (that doesn't involve a sales pitch)—all these and more are available to you. Take the opportunity to act.

Super doesn't only hold dinners around town and at tech conferences. He is involved throughout the community. He and I do many such things together because we both see the value in involvement and contribution to the industry.

Who do I call and promote internally within my company when we have a need? Yep. Super. Why? Not because he's a back-slapping buddy, but because he's built a solid relationship, contributes to the tech community, and has a good track record in his professional space.

Similar relationships are there for the making—all you have to do is get involved!

THE TAKEAWAY

Get involved in the tech industry, and you'll get more out of it than you put into it.

What's your networking pet peeve?

"Being stalked."

"People who won't take No for an answer."

"When you accept a LinkedIn invitation from somebody and immediately get flooded with follow-up emails, articles and constant communications."

"When people think they know about you because they've done a little research, but they bring up something you haven't worked on for three years."

"Being fake. We can always tell."

"Unknown salespeople using LinkedIn to schedule an hour-long call or meeting—tomorrow— because their schedule is free."

"Asking for my time to explain my challenges or business problems so they can figure out how best to articulate a value proposition. This is backward and never results in the response they desire."

The Ultimate Cheat Sheet on Getting in the Door

As a CIO who has spent 30 years in IT (15 years in IT sales and 15 years in executive IT management), I am somewhat of an expert when it comes to recognizing great IT sales talent. Unfortunately, I see very little of it these days.

Don't get me wrong: There are some good salespeople out there. But there are very few that I really look forward to meeting with when I see a meeting notice on my calendar.

I'm talking about the type of person who brightens your day when you see their number come up on your phone. The type of person who knows me and my business *before* they walk in the door. The type of person who brings real solutions to my problems, both business and technical, and offers a reality check on things my team and I are trying to accomplish. The best of the best will even admit when they don't have a solution for me, but still offer to help any way they can.

This is a true partnership.

There's an adage, "People buy from people they like." In IT sales, this is the golden rule. Your job as a salesperson for your company is to make me happy when you win and sad if you lose. Believe it or not, most CIOs really root for our favorite partners. When you do well, we win too. The best solutions, best pricing and best resources all go to clients that have a great relationship with their partners.

I've been asked numerous times what advice I'd give to sales execs trying to earn their way into my trusted inner circle. Let's start at the beginning.

Just as in any relationship, the first interaction is the key to a long, successful relationship. Think back to the first interaction you had with your best friend, significant other or spouse. You put some thought into what you were going to say before you approached them. You didn't run up and give them a 15-minute bulleted speech or PowerPoint presentation about why you were the best person to be their lifelong friend or partner. You put your best foot forward and did everything you could to get a conversation started.

It's the same way when you're approaching a new client at a prospective new account. You only get one chance to make a first impression.

I get an average of 40 to 50 emails and phone calls every day from vendors wanting to "get 15 minutes of my time" or "meet their senior executive who will be in town next Tuesday" or "solve all my problems while saving me 30% on my XXX budget." I don't read past the first line, and I don't listen past the first sentence of these types of general sales voice mails.

So, how do you get to me?

Here are the best ways to approach me and most CIOs:

- *Network:* Find someone who knows me and get them to introduce you. Not through LinkedIn (although that's better than nothing). Make it a face-to-face introduction at a conference or business lunch.

  When you first meet me, be prepared with your elevator pitch. In less than 30 seconds, tell me something that will make me want to meet with you a second time. Your goal for that first meeting should be to get a second meeting.

- *Event:* Do what you can to get me to attend an event where you can have that face-to-face introductory meeting. Meetings where other CIOs will be are a good start. However, understand that my main interest is meeting the other CIOs, so don't be too pushy. Make the event relevant for my industry. Bring in a respected industry spokesperson. Practice your elevator pitch and make it your goal to get the second meeting.

- *Email or voice mail:* Believe it or not, this *can* work. But you have to do your homework. Remember, I get a ton of these and give them about 10 seconds each before deleting. So, you have to get my attention in those 10 seconds.

You do this by doing some research on me and my company. Make the subject line something like "I see your IT spend is 4% of your company revenue. Did you know your competitor's is 3.2%? I have ideas on solving that." Or "I saw your presentation on IT security at [event]. On Slide 3 you mention remote offices. I have a way you could do that for a lower cost."

In other words, compel me to meet with you. Tell me something about my company, my industry, or even my own IT strategy that I didn't know before. I will be blown away and call you immediately. Even if you're wrong, it shows you have put thought into the meeting.

This is so easy to accomplish. All the information is at your fingertips on the internet. Most annual reports are available online. There is enough personal information on LinkedIn, Facebook, and other social media sites to get an idea of what I like, my hobbies, and my areas of interest. Personalize your message.

Starting the relationship off right is not a guarantee of success, but it goes a long way toward achieving your goals.

THE TAKEAWAY

Your relationship with a CIO starts with the first interaction. Make it a good one. Remember, you only get one chance to make a first impression.

CHAPTER 4

You've Got the Meeting. Now What?

YOU'VE PUT A LOT OF WORK into getting your first sales meeting with a CIO. Don't blow your big opportunity! From cookie-cutter presentations to lying sales reps, the CIOs we talked to have seen it all. In this chapter, we share CIOs' horror stories, pet peeves and "you won't believe it" moments from sales meetings gone wrong.

We'll also reveal how to make a meeting go right. (It's easier than you may think.) This is where all the homework you've done comes into play. Combine your knowledge of the prospect and your product or service with patience, politeness and professionalism, and you'll make a great first impression. Keep reading to find out what works—and what doesn't—in a sales meeting with a CIO.

Courtesy Ain't Old School; It's the Only School

Courtesy used to be commonplace. Always responding to invitations with an RSVP (well before the due date), opening the car door for your companion, or giving your seat on the train to a pregnant woman are gestures that show respect for others.

Whether courtesy is fading in society or not, it still matters in business relationships—and sometimes it matters a lot. Courtesy can salvage a bad situation and help you get another time at-bat. Forget courtesy, however, and all bets are off.

Case in point: Lucky Rep, who scored a lunch meeting with me, became Unlucky Rep in just 20 minutes by failing to display common courtesy.

I showed up at the appointed time, on time, and waited at the hostess desk. When the hostess inquired if I was waiting for others, I responded that I was meeting a party of two, as I knew Lucky was bringing a colleague along.

Five minutes go by. Ten minutes go by. No sign of Lucky.

I e-mail Lucky: "Are we meeting today? I'm at the hostess desk." No response.

At the 15-minute mark, I dig up an email from Lucky and spot a mobile number in the signature block. I call it. No answer.

By this time, I figured some emergency had popped up with Lucky, so I rushed to fetch some quick takeout to eat at the office before my next meeting.

I emailed Lucky while waiting for my takeout, explaining that I had waited 15 minutes, had emailed and called, and finally moved on to honor the rest of my commitments for the day.

I was disappointed, of course. Frustrated, yes. I was scrambling to get lunch before my next meeting. Never a great experience but, hey, it's not the end of the world. I was also hoping that nothing bad had happened to Lucky or to someone in Lucky's life.

Lucky evidently checked his email while I was waiting for my takeout. His responses came in fast and furious:

1. Lucky and colleague are sitting at a table, as they had been since 10 minutes before our appointed lunch time.
2. Lucky told me to call his cell phone—a different number than was listed in his email signature block.
3. Lucky was unsure why the hostess didn't bring me to his table.
4. Lucky forgot the cell phone listed in his signature block. It was back at the office.
5. Lucky said it was a shame and that we must reschedule.

Since this happened during prime NFL football season, let's go to instant replay and break it down:

- Lucky sat at the table for over 25 minutes and never once checked to see where I was. He didn't check email either.
- Lucky didn't carry the cell phone that he told me to call.
- Lucky trusted the hostess, a total stranger (and an obviously disorganized one at that) to bring the prospect (me) to the table.
- It's someone else's fault (the hostess) that we didn't connect.
- Now I'm supposed to allocate another meeting slot to Lucky.

What's missing? Courtesy. In just a few minutes Lucky showed me:

- Lucky wasn't focused on me at all. If you're not focused on me at a first meeting, how much can I expect that you will focus on me as a customer?

- Lucky really doesn't care if you can get in touch when you need to. That would be mighty frustrating if we were in the middle of a business deal.
- Lucky displayed poor judgment and lapsed attention at the initial meeting. It will be a frustrating relationship if that's Lucky's normal M.O.
- Lucky passes the buck. That means anything that goes wrong in our business relationship would be someone else's fault.
- Lucky doesn't respect my time. Lucky didn't apologize—ever. He simply assumed that I'd allocate time for another meeting.

I won't be a customer. There won't be a business deal. There won't be a business relationship. There won't even be another meeting. I won't take another chance on Lucky's M.O.

This was at least the third time in the last year a meeting was delayed or missed due to a sales rep not being present and accessible at the meeting spot. The trend is not at epidemic levels, but it's certainly increasing!

Salespeople work hard to get appointments. When you get one (perhaps by following some of the ideas in this book), you don't have to go overboard showing your gratitude, but don't take it for granted, either.

Imagine how good your guest feels when you are there in the appointed place at the appointed time, waiting for them, with an outstretched hand to shake.

Imagine how solid you feel when you know you've met your guest and can control the interaction, set the tone, and build rapport from the minute they walk in (and not leave it up to an absentminded hostess to do it for you!).

Simple, isn't it?

THE TAKEAWAY

Please, thank you, I apologize, and excuse me can go a long way, just like opening doors for your date went a long way back when you were dating. Courtesy matters. Use it, please . . . and thank you.

UNDERSTAND YOUR AUDIENCE

CIOs are very different from salespeople. We CIOs are more analytical and not as emotional as sales types. We depend on facts and figures because we are very process oriented. If a sales rep wants to connect with me, they need to do their homework, suggest a specific solution and get to the point. We don't respond well to "rah-rah" stuff.

It's Meeting Time. Use It Wisely

The Situation: Diligent Salesperson finally gets time with the CIO they've been pursuing for months on end. After trying everything, including emails, phone calls, and invitations to events, they finally hit on something that captured the CIO's attention and are now sitting at the same table with them.

What should Diligent do?

Option A

The clock is ticking, and Diligent's thinking goes like this:
Time's a-wasting and I must get my pitch out there to maximize the revenue potential from this very short time together!

- Diligent spends five minutes on pleasantries, then puts forth that always-awkward and overused line: "Let's talk about your roadmap to identify synergies."
- Conversation dies to a cordial exchange of points and ideas.
- If Diligent is lucky, something interesting comes up, but it's not guaranteed.

Option B

The clock is ticking, and Diligent's thinking goes like this:
This is the first meeting of what I hope will be many, so I must establish the basis of a relationship so I will get another meeting!

- Diligent spends whatever time it takes to get to know the CIO and allow the CIO to get to know them.
- They identify common interests. At some point the conversation turns to work and the matters at hand.
- The CIO and Diligent casually exchange concepts and ideas around needs and offerings.
- The CIO suggests a follow-up meeting to discuss more

details with the CIO's team.

Which clock are you listening to?

One clock ticks for the meeting; the other ticks for a lifetime.

You make the choice.

THE TAKEAWAY

Use your initial meeting time wisely to establish the foundations for a relationship, not to push for a transaction.

WHAT'S THE USE (CASE)?

What do you do when a CIO's organization isn't prepared for disruption, but the CIO is sensitive to hearing that? Walking in and telling someone they're unprepared is risky; you can't predict how they will react. But doing use cases can help them reach that conclusion themselves. Highlight parallel use cases within their industry or even cross-industry. "XYZ Company was facing such-and-such obstacles that they weren't prepared for; here's how we were able to help them."

Do You Want Fries with That?

I am currently running an enterprise software search process. With five major vendors and their partners in the mix, it's been an interesting study in different approaches to selling to the CIO.

Each of the five contestants has their own sales approach.

1. *McDonald's:* The biggest vendor has served millions. We line up and get their pitch and product, and we should be glad they served us. We'll get the same thing every other client gets, and we'd better like it. Service is greasy but passable; pricing is highly competitive. Nobody ever gets fired for ordering from them; Happy Meals all around. Their sales pitch: *We are the biggest; sign here.*

2. *Burger King:* Remember the "have it your way" campaign? This vendor can and will do whatever we want as long as we don't choose McDonald's. The product and price are OK, but they reek of desperation. They have some fans internally who just want to rebel against #1 and think flame broiling is better. Their sales pitch: *We are not #1; pleeease sign here*

3. *Chick-Fil-A:* This one serves up a different, better, industry-focused product (I must admit to a deep personal weakness for waffle fries). They are a potentially controversial choice and pricing is mid-range. However, they offer a really good product and service (and their seasonal milkshakes rock). Their sales pitch: *Service with a smile.*

4. *Hometown Buffet:* They have large quantities of every function you could ever want. Not a lot of service, but you can do it all yourself. They offer the cheapest price, all the basic functions, and the most options, which

means the CFO is lined up and ready to buy regardless of what the rest of us think. Their sales pitch: *Everything is at the buffet; pay at the front, please.*

5. *French Restaurant:* We should be honored that they let us ask them to bid on the project. They offer the highest price and fewest options, but we'll get top-flight service and functionality. Our internal sales team badly wants a table at this place and is ready to put it on the corporate credit card, *now*. Their sales pitch: *They can't be bothered to come out and make a pitch to the team. Instead, they took the CEO and head of sales to lunch.*

You know which one of these you are. I have no idea yet who is going to win my business, but can you spot the losers?

Here are some recommendations for each:

1. *McDonald's:* You got to be the biggest for a reason—and some of those reasons are why we won't choose you. Show us the benefits you offer beyond your size and make us want to start a relationship.

2. *Burger King:* Desperation is never a good approach. It's OK to be number two in a big market. Show confidence in your product and service. Compete on your own merit, not against everyone else.

3. *Chick-Fil-A:* Sure, the CIO is hungry, but make sure you know who your full audience is. Don't just cater to the project lead.

4. *Hometown Buffet:* Being the lowest-priced option is good, but it's never enough. The mix of service and product as also important. Show us how you strike a balance.

5. *French Restaurant:* There is merit in courting the key decision makers. However, this is a high-risk approach

that may alienate other influencers. In many companies, the decision process is more distributed. Find and engage the influencers, not just the top decision makers.

No product or sales team is perfect for every prospect. The key is to adjust, even if only slightly, to the prospect, and find out what they really need and how they decide. You should be glad we are considering you, so make it count.

THE TAKEAWAY

A one-size-fits-all sales approach won't work. Adjust your sales approach to the specific prospect.

It's Your First Meeting. Here's What *Not* to Do

You're preparing for a call tomorrow with a CIO you have never met before. You have 45 minutes to make a great first impression.

What do you say? What do you ask? How can you convince them that you and your company are worth doing business with?

I can tell you one thing not to do:

Don't ask them, "What keeps you up at night?"

You may not be immediately escorted to the door, but I assure you there won't be a second meeting.

CIOs and IT leadership can't stand that question. Instead of asking it, do your homework. The internet gives us unlimited information not only about the company but also about the person you're meeting with.

Take some time to read the company's annual report. Find out what the company's goals are and how IT needs to align with those goals. Ask a contact who has called on that CIO in the past. Do what you need to do to get the information.

—*The Super Salesperson*

THE TAKEAWAY

There are many ways to get information on a CIO and a company. Use them.

The Power of the Purchasing People

Salespeople need to understand that we are not only selling to the CIO or IT, but in many organizations, we are also selling to purchasing. The world has changed and often, and purchasing holds the purse strings.

Has this happened to you? Long sales cycle, lots of meeting and demos, and finally your internal champion (or even the CIO) says, "You are the vendor of choice."

You have won the technical battle. That's all good and a very important win, but now comes the cost negotiation.

You and your IT contacts enter discussions on cost in good faith. There's no reason to think these negotiations won't get you to a final contract and an agreed-upon price . . . is there?

"OK, now you have to go meet with Bob in purchasing." No problem, you think; this where the contract gets signed.

Except Bob needs his pound of flesh because that's what purchasing does. And oh, by the way, he also needs to know why IT needs the flux capacitor and the fetzer valve.

You're thinking "Did we just start the sales cycle all over again?"

What happens next? Your sale gets slowed down, you probably end up giving additional discounts that may require additional approvals within your organization, and you have to explain your solution and value to the company all over again.

How do you avoid this situation?

Ask upfront what role purchasing will play in the sales cycle. If necessary, have purchasing attend meetings during the sales cycle. Have them fully involved in the price negotiations with your contacts from IT. This approach ensures that IT and purchasing are on the same page.

—*The Super Salesperson*

THE TAKEAWAY

Purchasing plays a bigger role in the sales cycle than it used to. Know what the role of purchasing is before you start the process.

IMPROV TIME

The best meetings are the salespeople who can just "go with the flow." They don't get stressed out over having to finish the presentation or do the slides in order. They can throw the slide deck away and talk with us, being responsive to our questions. They can make it a conversation, not a sales pitch. That, to me, shows a well-oiled machine.

Want to Keep Your Job? Do This

Most salespeople do not know how to listen. In fact, they don't even know listening is something they should do.

I remember one of my first frustrating experiences with a sales professional. I still remember his name, his company, and his failure.

In his eyes and in the eyes of his employer, his only failure was that he didn't close the deal. However, since Kevin didn't know how to listen, he didn't hear me explaining that his product configuration didn't match my needs.

Kevin worked for "big tech." His sales pitch was scripted, and his demeanor was both professional and unshakeable. When I told Kevin I didn't want to buy his product the way it was configured and packaged, his response was to repeat the same statement over and over, as if repetition would eventually make it true (or make me see the light).

Kevin's employer created this environment, one in which Kevin was simply a powerless sales cog who had no flexibility to work with the customer. Kevin did not get it and probably has not to this day, 18 years later.

Kevin was soon removed from the account and another knight in shining armor arrived, promising me the world. In the last 12 months I've heard from three new reps from the company (Colleen, Anne, and now Joyce). Every new salesperson has the same story—and they are all "gone" come January.

As a salesperson, your role is to be the customer advocate inside your organization. You must build long-standing relationships, get to know the customer firm in detail, and be there to service the account, without any agenda other than to exceed the customer's expectations on the dimensions that matter.

If something is not right, your role is to go to bat for the customer, which means being willing to take risks and change.

THE TAKEAWAY

Listen to your customers so you can learn what matters to them.

Touch Your Phone, Kill the Sale

It happens all the time—but this time the tables were turned.

The prospect was texting during my entire presentation.

It took everything I had to keep my mouth shut and not say anything. It's hard enough to get these appointments. Do us a favor and at least pretend to be interested in what we are saying for 30 minutes.

We've all done it, me included. We're sitting at a presentation that we have seen before. We get a little bored, take our cell phone out and start reading emails, Facebooking, Tweeting, whatever.

I was attending a conference in Vegas this week and sat through several meetings in intimate groups. I noticed a recurring theme: Sales reps that couldn't put down their phones.

Guess what? The customer notices, and it pisses them off. It's just plain disrespectful. At that conference, I spoke to two CIOs who said they have disqualified vendors in the past just because of "the phone thing."

Putting your phone away for one hour will not kill you. If it's really an emergency, they'll have you paged.

Remember, keeping that phone in your pocket may be the differentiator that gets you the deal. Now isn't that easy?

—*The Super Salesperson*

THE TAKEAWAY

Never look at your phone during a meeting with a prospect or customer.

When Good Presentations Go Bad

We're about 20 minutes into a "pitch deck" meeting and the salesperson has yet to ask a question or engage with us. Has he even taken a breath? He's still talking about *his* company history, *his* clients, *his* product, and *his* success.

I stopped caring and started answering emails on my iPad about 12 minutes ago. He hasn't even noticed.

Why are we all in the room? Is it...

a) To finish the PowerPoint presentation regardless of all obstacles?

b) To bestow a lifetime achievement award on his company?

c) To test a new form of torture?

d) To determine if he has a *solution that meets my needs?*

If you answered anything but (d), you likely helped him write his presentation.

Unfortunately, most presentations I see are very similar. What do people (yes, prospects are people!) want to hear in a presentation?

- People want to be engaged, tell their story, and find a solution to their problems.
- They also tend to remember the first and last things you say or do—much of the middle is a blur.

Logic and experience tell us that if you merge the two ideas above, sales meetings should lead off and close with engagement. That looks something like this:

- Ask questions to verify that you understand the prospect's key needs.
- Then show specifically how you can solve them.
- Only present or speak to what is relevant to the prospect's needs.
- Know your material and your value so well that you can jump straight to the important stuff. Your pitch

deck should be backup, not the focus and objective of the meeting.

Open and close with engagement and dialogue, and you will be more successful. After all, you can't sell me anything if I stopped paying attention 12 minutes ago.

THE TAKEAWAY

Your presentation isn't about a PowerPoint. It's about engaging with a prospect and showing how you can solve their needs.

The Power of Common Ground

All salespeople have been there: Stuck on a sales call that's going downhill fast. Your services are not a fit, and you are squirming in your seat to find some common ground.

It happens.

Usually I do my research and find out something about the person before the meeting. I pride myself on being able to carry on a conversation with anyone.

This time I was in trouble. I'd done no research. I had no info. And there was no personality across the table.

No problem!

Out of the corner of my eye I saw a stuffed animal with the logo of a college near where I grew up.

Finally, a connection was established, and the sales call was salvaged.

Today, we should never be unprepared. There are so many avenues to find out about our prospects—Facebook, Twitter, LinkedIn, etc. Use these tools, and even if our products and services are not a fit for the prospect, at least we can bond about how our 14-year-old daughters drive us insane.

—*The Super Salesperson*

THE TAKEAWAY

Find a connection with the prospect, no matter how small.

Sell Them What They Need— Not What You Have

I was making a sales call this week and got some great advice:

Sell me what I need, not everything your company offers.

Sales folks like myself have many things in the toolkit to sell.

When we get the opportunity to sit down with a prospect, we get excited and want to let them know about *everything* we have to offer.

Bad idea!

In talking to CIOs I've received a consistent message:

Focus on my pain points and solve those problems first.

Do your homework. Get an understanding of the business and technical issues or challenges that are their current priorities. Sell them that first.

Present solutions, not just products. Teeing up a solution minimizes the need for detailed product evaluation. This saves valuable internal resource time and money. It can also speed the time to sale.

One CIO told me, "I had significant user experience issues. I had to put the fire out. I was looking for the vendor to wrap up the solution in a box and put a nice bow on it so I could pull the trigger and implement. Instead, what I got was a bunch of products for my team to evaluate. We didn't have time to do all that, so we pursued an internal solution."

Once you have achieved success with the point solution, the bing-bang will come down the road.

Budgets are tight and the pressure is on CIOs to provide immediate value to the business they support. Let's make them a quick hero, achieve trusted advisor status, lock out our competition—and enjoy a long, fruitful relationship with our customers.

—*The Super Salesperson*

THE TAKEAWAY

Provide solutions, not selections. Make it easy for the prospect to say yes.

Discover First, Prescribe Second

Imagine walking into the doctor's office and, instead of reading your medical records, taking your vital signs, looking in your ears (what *are* they looking for, anyhow?), and listening to your story, the doctor hands you a prescription and says, "Everyone has the flu right now; you must too. You need this medicine. Take it."

Would you fill the prescription?

Would you go to that doctor again? How would you feel?

Now, imagine meeting Jim. He's a sales leader for SMACmeUp.com (a fictitious company and URL).

Being with *the* leading firm in Social, Mobile, Analytics, and Cloud (*the* hot stuff these days), Jim's seen all the pain points of a wide range of customers. His solutions *are* the best. They have JPMorgan and Walmart on their customer roster. With those two names they *must* have a great product, right? Why don't *you* know about them already? He's sure that YOU have problems that HE can solve. All you need to do is listen to him.

He talks constantly. Every one of your intelligently probing questions, honed from years of experience so that you can understand his offering in terms that make sense to you, are deflected so he can tell you more about his successes.

What do you do?

Unfortunately, some people are in awe of Jim and bite on his approach.

Most people, however, don't like Jim. They tune him out.

Jim reflects on the call and how stupid you are for not calling him back. You reflect on the call and shake your head, thrilled that it's over and vowing to never take his call again. Unfortunately, Jim is just doing what he's been taught to do— and it's all wrong. Let's think about this for a minute:

How can people know my pain the minute they walk in the door? Are they clairvoyant? If so, why are they dwelling in the constant-rejection world of sales when they could be profitably trading the futures market?

Why do salespeople feel a need to paint us into a corner where we must have their stuff? Sales calls feel like a martial arts competition where I have to continually evade or deflect energetic blows. Not a great experience, trust me. And you won't get invited for "Round 2."

A good product sells itself. The trick to selling it is to get out of the way by making people feel comfortable with you, educating them at their level and, in the process, building a relationship. How do you do that?

My experience is that successful salespeople discover first and—only when they understand me, my company, and the situation—prescribe later.

Discovery is a way of building your knowledge base about a prospect or customer while at the same time building trust. It is not a questionnaire, it's a conversation at a measured pace.

Get to know them, just like you trust your doctors when they get to know you. You have to educate them on your product or service but do so in an easily digestible way. Most people are interested in learning something new. They just don't want it delivered via a beer bong. They have to taste it, savor it, and see if it's what they want, not just get drunk on it. If you do it right, they will be so educated and comfortable that they'll write their own prescription!

The best sales interactions I've had are with people who look to really understand me and my situation while allowing me to understand their offerings. That happens through an engaging discussion where, if nothing else, you make a friend, expand your network, hone your conversational skills, and grow your knowledge base. It's a win/win regardless of the sales outcome.

At some point in that conversation, we both realize that 1) it was nice meeting each other and we part ways wishing each other good luck with our pursuits, or 2) there's a potential match of need and solution and we should take it to the next level.

If you're going to the next level, that's where you can start testing options within the foundation of trust you've built on your way to a long-term, mutually beneficial relationship.

Try it. You might like it.

THE TAKEAWAY

Take some time to discover the problem and diagnose the patient before you prescribe a solution.

What's the worst meeting experience you ever had with a salesperson?

"A company we had done some work with the previous year came in with a proposal. They used the exact same pitch deck they'd shown us the year before—they just changed the title slide."

"The lead salesperson of a major software vendor yelled at their implementation team in front of us. It didn't make us want to come back for more."

"We invited a firm in for a meeting, and they could not stop telling bad jokes. It was like open mic night at a comedy club."

[A female CIO]: "I was in a meeting with the vendor, the salespeople, and two men from my team. The salespeople never made eye contact with me; at one point, they asked me to get them coffee."

"They brought in a PowerPoint with company logos of their clients. One was the logo of a company I founded and invested in. They claimed it was a major client. I knew that was a flat-out lie."

[A female CIO]: "During a sales call, the salespeople kept asking if I understood the 'technical stuff' or if I needed them to stop and explain it. They didn't ask any of the guys in the room this question."

"A guy opened the meeting by talking about politics."

Think Different

The biggest problems in meetings are cookie-cutter presentations and people who talk a lot. They're just two sides of the same coin: Salespeople who don't take the time to see things from the CIO's point of view.

In initial meetings, I respect salespeople who listen to us, probe, and ask questions. Only then do they suggest ideas for how their product could help.

Once they learn more about our needs by listening, salespeople can often make suggestions on how to introduce the product strategically, as opposed to implementing all at once. This can help make a sale to a company that's not ready for, or lacks the budget for, an enterprise-wide implementation. Tailoring your solution for where the customer is now is impressive. It shows you're willing to give up some short-term commission to build a relationship for the long term.

The bigger problem: Many salespeople, especially younger ones, don't understand the magnitude of the CIO's job. They don't realize that it is not about the nuts and bolts of technology so much as it is about knowing the business, aligning the business, and thinking strategically.

You have to be strategic about selling to the CIO. Instead of telling me lower-level things about the product features, tell me how it will help me strategically. Show me how other companies have used it and what ROI and results they got. The features of your technology are not as important as the business aspect—what your product can do for me strategically.

That's why it's important to have the right people in the room from both sides, both the vendor and the client side. Technology purchases are big, complex systems and big decisions involving many people. The CIO sees the high-level view, but people under the CIO care about the nuts and bolts.

Having both of them in the room is how deals get done.

THE TAKEAWAY

If you want to sell to a CIO, think like a CIO when preparing for your meeting.

Are You Throwing Away Free Money?

We were facing a renewal of a major equipment services contract with a national vendor. Let's call them Koncorp.

Before bidding it out, we decided to start with Koncorp and give them the first shot at the renewal. We had not called for service in a long time since the product was very stable. They were essentially getting free money.

We were clear up front that this was a chance to keep us from bidding the contract out, but still Koncorp managed to drop the ball in every possible way.

Want to learn a lesson from Koncorp? Here's how *not* to retain a current customer at renewal time:

- They didn't approach us before renewal. We had to hunt for them.
- They couldn't provide an accurate schedule of current contracted services. (We had one, but I always ask the renewing vendor for this information, and they had no current records.)
- We told them we wanted to evaluate the platform and plan for the future. Instead of asking about our projected needs, they just emailed us a pricing sheet (list price, no discount, which was higher than the current pricing) for the services we already had.
- The sales rep left me a voicemail at 11:40 am telling me to call him if I did *not* want his entire local office team to show up at my office at noon. After showing up without an appointment, they gave our receptionist a hard time for not hunting me down or letting them into my suite. She did her job well in keeping them at bay.
- When I expressed dismay at all the above to their local management, the account moved from my local rep to a national call center. Because I was not a quick and easy

renewal win on their terms, they demoted me.

Needless to say, we eliminated them from consideration, and we moved the business to one of their major competitors.

The irony is that the competitor is charging me more than Koncorp, but also upgraded the services because they identified my new, real need. The competitor won because they showed me greater value and met my needs. They also won because Koncorp blew it.

The cost of acquiring a new customer is massive. Renewals are relatively inexpensive and a measure of the quality of your product or service. But you should never treat renewals as slam-dunk, low-effort revenue. Instead:

- Know what you are providing and show how you can add even more value.
- Start the renewal process well in advance of the contract dates by meeting and planning with your client.
- "Blend and extend" your contract into the renewal, if possible—don't give them a chance to wander.
- Woo me like a new customer during the renewal.

It's simple: I just want to know you still care about my business and respect our relationship.

THE TAKEAWAY

Never treat renewals as a slam-dunk. Give them the same attention you'd give to a new sale.

"What Do You Think?"

I am in the midst of building a new business, and my firm has created offerings I hope will resonate with my customers.

We have spent countless hours on our approach, documentation and sales pitch. We have talked to many people, gotten suggestions, and have gone to market with offerings we think the IT world will love.

Guess what? Stuff happens, and what you thought was a terrific offering may only suit a portion of the market.

In every meeting I have with senior IT leadership types, I always leave time to get their perspective on what I am selling.

These folks are living and breathing it every day. They are the ones who matter—and their *opinion* matters.

It may be hard to hear that your solution is not a fit, but we live in a time where you must be willing to listen and change your approach as the market changes.

A great example of this happened to me on a recent sales call.

I was meeting with an IT leader who's been doing this for a lot longer than me. We discussed a new offering my company created, and I asked him his thoughts on our approach. He was delighted to add his perspective and offer a different way to potentially sell it.

Guess what? When we make the changes, I'll head right back to him to get his opinion—and hopefully make him a customer.

—*The Super Salesperson*

THE TAKEAWAY

Take the time to ask the customer their opinion. They are the reason we exist.

CHAPTER 5

Closing the Sale

YOU'VE COME SO FAR—and you're nearly at the finish line. You can almost smell that commission! Don't get cocky: There are still many ways things can go wrong before the deal is sealed.

Is another vendor undercutting you on price? Are there so many decision-makers you can't keep them straight? Are your emails and voicemails to the prospect going into a blackhole—and the end of your quarter is coming up? In this chapter, we reveal do's and don'ts for getting over these and other common hurdles to closing the sale.

5 Must-Do's After Your Next Sales Demo

Demoing, like your golf swing, is as much about follow-through and maintaining your form after you strike the ball, as it is about setting up your shot.

If your post-demo track record has been a letdown, it could be that you're placing too much emphasis on that single event to clinch the sale. Just like that golf swing, your strategy may need to involve tracking where the "ball" is going and following it up the course, instead of just going for a hole-in-one.

Here are five important things to do after you demo your product.

1. *Be proactive and anticipatory about opportunities to close.*
   Golf courses give you 18 opportunities to get your ball into that hole. There are many players on all the holes, playing simultaneously. Consider your buyer's corporate culture, timeline and decision-making process not only before the sale, but also during and after. There may be trigger events that move your product or service into, or out of, a top priority spot. Are you ready to act on these factors and impact their decision to buy?

2. *Continue to involve your sales engineer in your selling process.*
   Too often, the sales engineer is taken off the shelf, dusted off, thrust in front of the client to demo and answer technical questions, and then retired back to the shelf until the next demo. When you work with your sales engineer as a team from start to finish through post-sale support, you both have a better chance of understanding your customer's business mindset. Debrief with each other frequently. Grow each other's sales and engineering brains. In a sense, you are both playing and caddying with each other.

3. *Identify additional opportunities within your clients' cultures.*
   If you are taking turns playing and caddying, it could be

that the selling process sometimes resembles a scramble. Which one of you, salesperson or sales engineer, is in the best position to identify new leads within prospect organizations? While you are focusing your efforts on one group, your golfing team partner may identify other folks who can benefit from your product or service. Then your relationship with your prospect becomes a matter of a multi-license or product sale, instead of a single sale. That shift in how you and your sales engineer are regarded by your prospect may make your solution a priority for them.

4. *Develop your prospects as information resources.* Keep your eye on the ball and never forget you are playing on a golf course. After the demo, there's a tendency to make every discussion you have with that prospect into one which, ultimately, asks a spoken or unspoken question: *How close are you to deciding to buy?* But post-demo conversations are also an opportunity to showcase your own and your sales engineer's business acumen. Talk industry and regulatory trending and ask your prospect's opinion of how these triggers are impacting their own business development strategies. Partner with them as they and their company play on the same golf course.

5. *Complete the course together.* When your selling strategy involves collaboration among you, your sales engineer and your customer's team, you all get to the finish line together. Do the tools (or "golf clubs") that you are selling provide the best means of addressing how your customer is going to play on their globally competitive business "golf course"? You may not have the optimal solution. However, if your tools provide the most robust, yet flexible, strategies for solving that specific prospect's problems, then you have earned their business and an ongoing spot on their team.

THE TAKEAWAY

Doing the demo doesn't mean you've made the sale. Be sure to follow through to the close.

HELP THE CIO CLOSE

No matter how small an organization you work for, the CIO still has to "sell" any new purchase internally. Good sales reps know that and will craft an approach that helps the CIO spin a better story for their stakeholders.

It Takes a Village

As sales professionals, the power to close the sale sometimes depends on others.

For those of us that have Type A personalities, having to lean on or trust someone else to get the deal done makes us sick. We like to be in control.

Too bad!

It's time to move on and get over it. Embrace, and ask for, the help.

As sales cycles become longer and what we are selling becomes more complex, we must lean on others to help make the sale happen.

If you work for a larger company, you have a team of resources available. Use them!

I miss the days when I had SMEs at my disposal. These folks can really help you close the business if they're prepared and put in the right situation. It's up to you to coach them.

Those of us in smaller companies with fewer resources must get creative and do the extra homework to make sure we are prepared. Not an easy task, but it's what we signed up for.

—*The Super Salesperson*

THE TAKEAWAY

If you want to get the sale, ask for help.

How to Handle a Long Sales Cycle

Long sales cycles spell opportunity for salespeople who know how to use that time wisely. If you know it will take a while for your product or service to get through a prospect's buying process, invest that time in getting to know that customer.

Get to know our business and know who we are. Get to know our roadmap. Learn where the CIO's pain is and where it is not. Be able to articulate how your product or service fits into our ecosystem. Start building a relationship.

Once you know your product or service is relevant to the CIO's needs, other things you can do during the long sales cycle are:

- *Learn who the stakeholders are in the organization.* Who's the decision maker? Who's a contributor? Who's an influencer?
- *Know where the CIO has leverage and where they don't.* If procurement is involved, or if everything goes through a lengthy RFP process, there's usually a point where the CIO feels like they don't have any leverage. Help them get through that point in the decision-making process by building relationships with the other stakeholders yourself.

  If I think a vendor may become a strategic partner in products and services with us, I introduce them to our procurement group, our legal group and our contracts group. Then the salesperson can start to educate my peers and vice versa.
- *Help build real business cases.* CIOs don't want fictitious "We can save you $3.5 million in cost avoidance," but real, hard dollars on the P&L business cases.

Those are the building blocks. If you want to level up from that and really make a good impression, offer training and certification before the sale ever gets close to closing. Offer a POC.

A lot of times you'll try to set up a POC with a services company, and they'll have all these reasons why they can't do it. It's the salesperson who figures out a way to make it happen that that gets the sale. That means when you get to the actual execution and contract stage, the adoption and implementation cycle is shortened tremendously.

Get buy-in. Some salespeople mistakenly think the CIO unilaterally makes decisions about products or services. That's not how it works. Any CIO is going to turn to their team and ask "What do you think?" Any decision an IT executive makes without the buy-in of the team is a bad decision. Providing training, certification and POC are a big part of getting that buy-in.

What *not* to do during a long sales cycle:

- *Don't accelerate a deal that's not able to be accelerated.* Often, this is something that's not budgeted. For instance, if we're in Q3 of my fiscal year, I need to work with the vendor on the sales cycle to come up with a number and put it in the budget for the following fiscal year. Instead, some vendors push that sale and try to close that deal prematurely.

  If I'm not going to have the money until next year, you would be a lot better off if you came to the table looking like you wanted to partner with us and doing it on our terms vs. just trying to close a sale. Salespeople who try to close deals as they near the end of a fiscal quarter or a fiscal year are incredibly annoying. Others will say they're willing to wait it out, but only want to do so until their financial junctures. That's just as bad.

- *Don't upsell me on the next product before I've bought*

the first one. During a sales cycle where we've been going for six or nine months, doing an RFP, building requirements and demoing, salespeople often get a little bit antsy and try to upsell me on another product. They're smooth about it: "Hey, here's a great opportunity. I know we were working on X, but Y would really dovetail nicely into that, so why don't we package them both together?"

Hold your horses! Before I buy Y, I need to buy X. I need to get it implemented. You need to prove that you can work with us, and we need to prove that your product works. All this needs to happen before we start buying add-on modules, other products or additional capabilities.

- *Don't try to go around a stakeholder.* Once a vendor who knew my purchasing authority was $1 million was trying to sell us something that cost $1.8 million. They tried to break the deal down into two $900,000 deals so I could sign them. Something like that is easy to see through and will backfire on you.

    Most CIOs are very explicit with the salesperson about the buying cycle and the process. Trying to skirt that in any way, shape or form leaves a bad taste in the CIO's mouth.

There are three or four vendors in my IT partner ecosystem. Regardless of the length of the sales cycle, they are extremely vested in our company. Even when they're not selling anything, they offer us additional training and certification or stop in to do a lunch-and-learn on their dime. They're part of who we are. That's what a long sales cycle can do for you—if you know how to use it.

THE TAKEAWAY

A long sales cycle can be a gift if you use the time wisely to get to know your prospect and truly partner with them.

HANG IN THERE: THE CALL'S COMING

It's been one of those weeks. No one you talk to or get in front of seems to care about what you are selling. We all hit that wall occasionally. Being a sales rep in IT is not an easy gig. You need to create value and differentiate yourself from the hundred other companies that sell similar products. The key to winning this rat race is persistence (and hopefully a product or service that folks need). If you do the right things, keep their attention, and act in a respectful manner, they will call. It may not be today, tomorrow, or next week, but it will happen.

How Can I Miss You If You Won't Go Away?

I'm in the middle of evaluating several products for a major project we have planned. We've had the demos and the discussions, exchanged NDAs and boilerplate contracts. Now it's down to decision time.

This is a time I like to reflect on the need, the options and the possibilities. I will call or email the vendor if I have a thought or a question. This is *not* a time where I need to know the vendor's exact location within three feet.

Then why are sales reps emailing and calling to give me hourly updates on their location, activity and availability? Why would I possibly need to know they are "down the shore," "picking up the kids from camp," or "sitting in the airport?" I don't even know where my own children are with this much precision, and I care about my kids.

These travelers tell me they want to be available "just in case" to answer questions, address issues, and, of course, sign the contract. With smartphone in hand and the breathless readiness of a heart surgeon ready to be called for a transplant, they feel I need to know in real time their location and availability to drop everything to serve me.

Let's assume two things:

1. Your cellular service and email capabilities are working perfectly, since you are using them to file these unwanted travel logs.

2. If I leave you a voice mail or wait a bit for your response to an email, this is a normal part of business and just fine since we are not performing brain surgery or landing a spacecraft on Mars.

If both these assumptions are correct, what is your motive? Desperation, pressure, insecurity, boredom? None of those sound like my problem or an enticement to closing the deal. I don't really care where you are when you answer the phone, read my email, or respond to my voice mail—and by constantly updating me, you're just annoying me into picking a different vendor.

It really is simple (and much less work) to get this right. Only contact me if you have important information or action items. I will call you if I need anything—and I'll call if I'm ready to close the deal.

THE TAKEAWAY

Modern technology makes connecting easy—sometimes, too easy. Don't annoy the CIO into dropping you from consideration.

SHORT-TERM PAIN, LONG-TERM GAIN

In every single implementation, there will be surprises, pain points and things nobody thought of. For the salesperson to do the right thing when that happens requires advocating on behalf of the customer inside the organization. That might be painful; it might not be economically advantageous in the short term. But when you take the short-term pain on behalf of the customer, you earn a long-term relationship.

Dealing With the Summer Slowdown

Around the 4th of July weekend, the official start of summer (and no one calling you back) begins.

To me, this is a great time of year to unwind, relax a little, and solve the world's problems.

What it's *not* a great time for is selling anything.

It's hard for us sales folk to remain patient this time of year, but we must. Keep your cool as your customers and prospects take a little break.

Why aren't they calling us back? Not because they can't stand us (OK, maybe they can't stand some of us), but because they are on the beach or at the lake or on a flight enjoying their vacations.

How will your prospect feel if the little bit of vacation they get each year is constantly interrupted by your emails, texts and voice mails "checking in" or "touching base" on your proposal? Do you think they'll remember you fondly? When they're reminiscing over vacation photos of their kids on the beach, will they say, "Gee, I'm sure glad Sales Guy Dave called me right then"?

Busy CIOs don't get a lot of time off. Why not let them savor it?

Give your prospects a break during the summer slowdown. Let them recharge. It's only for a few weeks, after all. And when they get back, they'll be a little more relaxed, a little happier, and a little more sympathetic to getting you that PO or SOW before the quarter ends.

—*The Super Salesperson*

THE TAKEAWAY

Don't hassle your prospects during their downtime. Let them enjoy it.

What's one thing a salesperson did that blew the sale?

"We were almost ready to buy, but there were still a few steps to go through. They went above my head to my boss."

"They brought in a really annoying salesperson who offended a business stakeholder."

"I was negotiating with a salesperson and their other sales reps kept calling my admin, saying I should be dealing with them instead. Internal competition from their own company torpedoed that sale."

"With a deal essentially closed, the salesperson's manager insisted on meeting with me. His personality completely turned me off. He did nothing but talk about himself, how successful he's been and his career at various well-known companies. We moved on from that deal—not solely for this reason, but it didn't help the cause."

Get by With a Little Help from Your Friends

We sales folks can't catch a break.

We spend weeks, months, sometimes years trying to close deals.

The customer finally says yes.

Then guess what?

We take it back to the office, and the powers that be tell us "We can't accept this deal."

What?! Are you crazy?

I learned early on in my selling career that selling internally was the key to my success. This is especially important if you're working for a big company. You must find those champions in your organization who understand the true meaning of "Nothing happens until I sell something."

Translation: "If I don't sell anything, you won't have a job, Mrs. Attorney, Mr. Marketing Dude, Ms. HR Director, Mr. VP of who knows what."

So many people think salespeople make all the money while they are slaving away back at the home office. I can't tell you how many times I've wanted to say, "There's a sales job open; why don't you come give it a whirl?"

Selling doesn't stop when you make the sale. Find the folks within your organization that appreciate what salespeople do. More important, make friends with the people who can make things happen internally. It will pay off in the long run.
—*The Super Salesperson*

THE TAKEAWAY

Selling internally is just as important as selling to the customer.

Take This to Your Leader

One of the biggest challenges for a salesperson is managing the full team in an enterprise contract bidding and RFP process.

Let's set the scene: Recently, I've been focused on creating scale and flexibility for our company. To that end, we have bid out our core infrastructure, including cloud and managed services for that platform. Our objective is to partner (note that word) with a company that can help expand our business capacity with a better platform.

The frontline sales rep (let's call him Joe) is someone with whom I have a long relationship, but his company was recently acquired by another. The good news is that this gives Joe an expanded arsenal of products and capabilities. The bad news is that it brings a new company president . . . who just eliminated Joe's company from the bid with one phone call.

Yes, salesperson Joe brought in the opportunity by building trust and a relationship with me, and the new company president just blew it in less than 15 minutes.

We were down to four companies, who were making final presentations. Joe's new company president (let's call him Dan) swooped into the evaluation and demo process and made several major blunders that cost his company the deal:

- Dan called and emailed me demanding a lunch or dinner meeting that week that worked with his "very busy" schedule (not mine). Instead, I warily scheduled a call for a time that fit my schedule better. I liked their bid and really wanted to see deeper into the newly changed company.
- When we finally had that call, Dan had clearly not prepped with Joe. Dan launched right into the elevator speech. He then steamrolled along with a vision of

how I would outsource my entire team to him within 18 months. He wrapped the monologue by explaining how I should be honored to be on their platform.

- Dan clearly explained to me how any vision different from his own was career suicide for me or anyone in my position. (Thankfully, he was here to help me keep my job.) Dan also offered, unsolicited, to provide references within our shared network that would verify his vision. He offered to have his assistant schedule the deal closing and signing dinner for the next week. Dan then explained that he was "very busy," bid me good day, and hung up.
- Still stunned from the call, I got immediate emails from Dan introducing me to the references I never asked for.

Dan never asked me one real question during the call.

He never checked to find out what my goal or vision was (even though it was clearly stated in the RFP and we had been talking with Joe for two months about the project).

I was grateful that I didn't have to spend a full lunch or dinner listening to this pompous windbag.

I felt invaded. The whole process was clearly about him, not about my company or my need.

Our peaceful RFP process had just been set ablaze by the leader of one of the parties.

I eliminated the company from the RFP almost immediately. It was painful to explain to my friend Joe that he did not lose on price or product; he lost because I never want to talk to his company president again.

It's vital to have all key people in your company on the same page during the sales process. You should all be focused on the customer and prepared for all interactions. Don't let your company leadership invade during a peaceful negotiation!

THE TAKEAWAY

Tell your leadership that they are an important part of the sales process, but that they should follow your lead. After all, you are the one who paved the road to this sale.

DISAPPEARING ACT

Do you stay engaged with the prospect from the pre-sale phase all the way through to the implementation? As a CIO, I find it frustrating when companies transition personnel from pre-sales, to implementation, and to technical support. The disconnects between these teams are obvious and very disruptive. Often, the folks downstream of the sales rep are clueless about my business goals and all the needs I already shared with the sales team. When the sales rep does their song and dance and then disappears, it's bad for the relationship and for the sale.

What's one thing a salesperson did that clinched the sale?

"We were on the fence about buying because it was a new technology and we weren't sure we wanted to take the risk. Their CEO came to the sales meeting, made a commitment that they would stand behind it and ensure our success, and wrote that into the agreement."

"Being flexible on pricing and able to make an offer—vs. saying, 'Oh, I have to go back to my boss to check on that'— can clinch a sale right in the meeting."

"We were kind of nervous about the technology, and they gave us an uplifted support plan at no charge. They took away our fear by showing they were going to stand behind their products and make sure we were successful."

"A big, pending deal was coming up. The vendor's fiscal year-end was looming, but the salesperson never once mentioned trying to close the deal before then. That showed it was all about the partnership and the client, not their P&L."

"We were trying to close a multi-million-dollar deal before the pricing expired at the end of the quarter, but it was summer and we didn't have the resources to turn around the documents fast enough. The salesperson told us if we made a good-faith effort, the pricing would not expire even if we didn't meet the deadline. Because they took the pressure off, we actually met the deadline."

"When I know I'm in the market for something and I've put out a competitive RFP, a really good presentation or compelling financial offer can clinch the deal."

Trust Your Gut—Not Your Management

I can't tell you how many times over my sales career some upper management type, who doesn't know my territory, probably doesn't even know my name, and certainly doesn't know my customer, has asked me to do something that made absolutely no sense to get a deal closed.

We salespeople are the ones who build the relationships on the ground. We have spent countless hours educating prospects about our products, and in many cases befriending these folks.

Does some spreadsheet jockey who sits at a desk calling us at all hours of day and night really know better than we do what our next move should be?

Guess what? They don't!

I have seen it play out too many times: A salesperson succumbs to a manager who forces us to ask the customer to do something that will ultimately ruin the relationship we have built.

Do yourself a favor: Trust your gut. If your gut says no, don't do it.

We change jobs an average of eight times during our career. If you continue in the sales field, you will most likely be selling to the same prospect again—and it's not worth jeopardizing the relationship. Don't let the spreadsheet jockey make the call.

—*The Super Salesperson*

THE TAKEAWAY

Trust your gut. You're the one who knows the customer—not your manager.

Are You a Partner or Just a Vendor?

At my company, we talk a lot about the difference between vendors and partners. *Vendors*, we buy stuff from; *partners*, we're in business with.

- A *vendor* wants to sell as many widgets as possible, and they want to sell on their cycle to meet their pipeline demands.
- A *partner* wants to deliver as much value as possible, and they do it on our cycle to meet our demands.

Salespeople should want to be partners, but many of them are perfectly satisfied being vendors.

A *vendor* is the person who sends me the same email 15 times, doing a "reply" each time so I get the entire thread.

A *partner* is the person who invests the time to understand my needs and my industry.

Most salespeople who approach us have more than one product or service they can offer. Before calling or coming in, think through how your product or service could be adapted into my existing universe.

You should be able to say, "I don't know everything about your firm, but here's how we've adapted this particular solution—one of many that my company offers—to companies like yours," then give me two minutes on that topic (not 10). That's a way to create interest without knowing a lot about my company specifically.

If you're a vendor, can you ever become a partner? Yes, but it takes a change in mindset.

A vendor had been doing a certain type of equipment installation and support for many years. They were doing a poor job, so we had relegated them to vendor mode. The only reason we kept dealing with them was that they had custom-programmed the equipment, and it would be very difficult and expensive to have someone else take it over.

Then there was a management changeover at that firm. We met with the new management and were very open about the problems. We also copped to the fact that we as a company had not always been a good client. That's important in going from vendor to partner: If you want to have a good partner, you have to be a good client.

I asked if we could reset the relationship. I said, "I will work hard and have our team work hard to be good clients to you, but you've got to work very hard to become a good vendor to us."

Transforming the relationship required the partners on both ends coming together, putting our cards on the table, giving and taking feedback, making and keeping commitments, and doing that repeatedly and reliably.

Over the next year, they went from being a vendor—and a vendor that we wanted to get rid of, no less—to a very desirable partner. They participated in the redesign of equipment and systems for a new headquarters we're building. Now we go out to dinner, we talk shop, they've introduced other potential services to us, and we're very comfortable doing so because I know they're operating in a spirit of partnership. Of course, any relevant services they offer us has to rise or fall on its own merits. But now the door is wide open thanks to the investment of time, effort and commitment they made.

Of course, a partner can also become a vendor. It's never a happy event when that happens.

We had a partner that had hundreds of people engaged with us doing over $10 million worth of work. But as a result of that relationship, they felt fat and happy. They began to miss commitment after commitment after commitment and just gave us lip service. They thought it would be too difficult for us to leave them, and they became overconfident.

It wasn't too difficult. Today, we still do a little bit of business with them, but it's hundreds of thousands of dollars annually, down from over $10 million a year. They went from a partner to a vendor, all because they felt they were too big to fail.

THE TAKEAWAY

Some salespeople are partners. Some are just vendors. Which will you be?

MONEY MATTERS

When deciding between two vendors, close price parity is important. Of course, when you're talking about a $10 million deal, I'm not going to pick one vendor over another based on a $30,000 difference in price. But if we're paying a premium, there needs to be a clear understanding of what we're getting for it.

How to Win the Sales Competition

You've been working on this sale for months. It's a big one. And now it's down to you and one or two other competitors. How do you ensure you're the one crossing the finish line? Let me tell you.

Once we're down to a few finalists, I know that both companies could deliver the product or service. Now it's about how you recommend we implement your solution.

The winners are willing to admit that they don't know what they don't know. They'll say, "I'm not sure. Let's agree to a four- to six-week 'phase zero,' where we really dig into what you're trying to do. Then we'll come back and give you a firm recommendation."

The losers say, "Don't worry. We've done this a million times before. If we win the deal, we'll take care of you." They don't give me enough detail. They don't take into consideration that our company may not do it the way the rest of the industry does. They don't ease my fears.

When I'm buying a new solution, I'm typically talking to you about something I don't know how to do, so I'm looking for someone to make sure we're successful. If you're one of a couple finalists, it's not what your product does that sways me. It's whether you give me the confidence you're going to get me to the outcome I'm trying to achieve.

Show me you're not just going to drop the product off at my doorstep. You're going to work with me side by side. You're not going to nickel and dime me on implementation and training. I'd rather have a single price that includes those things than find out later that every time I reach out to customer support I get charged.

It's also important to show me that you are part of a team. I realize salespeople don't know everything about my industry or even about their own companies. I'm not looking for a salesperson to be my single point of contact. I'm looking for them to be an effective general contractor for their enterprise and pull in the subcontractors, if you will, that can really deliver and work together.

Demonstrate that you can navigate your organization and you have the authority and the power to bring the right people to the table. If you bring in a well-integrated series of subcontractors and people throughout your organization, and they prove they can work together on implementation, that is powerful to me.

At the end of the day, if two solutions can work, I'm going to go with the one that shows they really care about me.

THE TAKEAWAY

Winning the sale isn't about what your product or service does. It's about what you will do to make it work for the customer.

Give Me a Sign

How do salespeople know when the CIO is ready to buy? It's not hard: We give you plenty of signs.

- Are they enthusiastic?
- Are they asking a lot of questions?
- Are they doing a lot of follow-up?
- Have they brought other folks from their team into the mix to get their views on whatever it is that they're going to purchase?

It all boils down to engagement. Engagement is the biggest sign that a salesperson is in a good position.

Of course, we CIOs also give you signs when we aren't ready to buy. Again, it all boils down to engagement.

- Is the CIO ignoring your calls?
- Are they not answering your emails?
- Do they seem uninterested in what you have to say?
- Have you given them a price and you're still getting no response?

This lack of engagement is a good indicator that they're either not ready to buy now or they're not going to buy at all. It also could be a red flag that there's competition and you haven't been chosen.

Knowing if CIOs are ready to buy is straightforward. But sometimes salespeople create a problem where there isn't one. That's because sales folks have a quota to make. So even when they're in a good position, they sometimes try to force the sale before it's ready to close. They want to make something happen unnaturally fast, instead of allowing time for it to be thought through, properly vetted, and put through the right channels for the purchase to happen.

If you don't understand the buying process at a customer company, you can kill the sale even when the client plans to

buy. You need to know:
- Who is the ultimate decision maker?
- What is the process?
- What is the typical timeline? If something has to go through legal review, will that take 48 hours or two weeks?
- Who are the other folks in the approval chain? Are any of them unavailable?

When salespeople know how the client's buying process works and how long it takes to get from "I'm ready to buy" to executing the purchase, they can set expectations with their management. You know that you still need Fred's approval but he's on vacation for another week or that the contract will be in legal review for a month.

Unless there's something deadline-driven, the customer doesn't have to get the deal done in a certain period of time. They're not under the same pressure as a salesperson is. The best way to handle this discrepancy is to put together a mutual success plan so that each party, the vendor and the customer, understands the process that has to take place to get this done. Clarify all the steps and put them on a timeline them so you're both on the same page.

THE TAKEAWAY

Even when your client is ready to buy, pushing too hard can kill the deal. Understand your client's buying process to stay in the game.

The Sale Doesn't Stop After the Close

Do you think that the signing of ink and clearing objections is the terminal point of our relationship? If so, you've already lost me. If I can sniff out that attitude during the sales process, you're probably not going to make it to post-sale.

As CIO and CMO of several companies for the past decade, I apply a life-cycle view of the customer to my relationships with salespeople. The post-sale side of the transaction is part of the customer life cycle—a big part.

But probably less than a quarter of companies are good at post-sale service—and that may be an overly generous estimation. How can you make sure you're among the few and the proud?

- *Don't ghost me.* Sometimes the sales rep disappears immediately. I'm handed over to the sale team, and I never see the salesperson again.
- *Don't try to upsell me.* As soon as I buy, the salesperson is already working on the next transaction. "I've got 20 other things I can sell you," they say, knowing full well you don't really need any of them.
- *Do be a partner in service.* My best vendors come back and check in to make sure that the product delivery lives up to what they promised in the contract. "Are we hitting the service level agreement? Are you getting callbacks in a timely matter? Have we dealt with any problems you have with implementation?" They may not be involved day to day, but they're making sure that the day-to-day experience is what they promised it would be.

Want to really stand out at post-sale? Get the support team involved pre-sale. Bring them to the sales meetings. After all, these are the people who will take care of the customer day to day, after the ink dries and the check clears. Why not help the customer develop a relationship with them?

Bringing in the support team during the sales process also shows me if there's a good working relationship. When the conversation and body language show that salespeople and support people get along, that's a good sign. Conversely, if it's clear that these people are never in a room together and don't particularly like each other, that can knock a vendor out of the running.

More than once, I've bought a product even though I didn't like the sales rep because I was blown away by the support people. Showing me that the people we'll be dealing with for the next three to five years are people I can trust matters more than the effectiveness of the salesperson.

Why is post-sale service so important? Every contract comes up for renewal. Eventually, I'll be evaluating the next generation of software, renewing or expanding the service agreement or replacing the hardware.

More important, I'm going to get a call from one of my friends who's going to say, "Hey, we're looking at XYZ company, and we saw that you're a customer. Do you recommend them?"

Post-sale to me is pre-sale to my colleague down the street who's calling me to ask whether they should trust you. The cycle never ends. Yes, I expect ongoing care and feeding—but if you deliver, it will pay off.

THE TAKEAWAY

Every post-sale experience is also a pre-sale, either to that customer or to someone they know. Don't drop the ball.

CONCLUSION

Be a Professional

THROUGHOUT THE EARLY MODERN PERIOD, only three professions were recognized by society: medicine, law and religion. The criteria for these "learned professions" involved a formal education, extensive training, and fees paid for services rendered.

Over time, the list was amended to include occupations such as accounting, engineering and nursing, but not sales. Never sales.

That's all changing.

In 2012, Harvard Business School (HBS) hosted the inaugural conference on thought leadership in the sales profession. The innovative event brought together academicians and sales practitioners to give meaningful weight to sales (and sales management) practitioner interests and actively connect academics to these interests.

Mind you, HBS didn't manufacture the interest in this subject matter; it was merely responding to the groundswell. Indeed, independent and student-led events on campus that focus on sales and sales management are gaining in popularity. But there's still a long way to go.

Higher education (aka academia) isn't doing CIOs any

favors by sending graduates to the front lines with so little exposure to sales. A quick scan of the top-rated business schools in the U.S. reveals a shocking indifference toward undergraduate sales education. If you're an aspiring sales professional, you have to enroll in your respective university as a marketing major and hope to get one course that addresses sales. Unfortunately, that one course is typically tucked away in the basement and taught by someone who never worked in sales. At the graduate level, it's even worse.

Could our lack of a "formal" education be the reason we're viewed as hucksters of snake oil and/or used cars? Without the appropriate formal instruction on our resume, why should we be viewed any differently?

This oversight in academia forces sales professionals to earn their "diplomas" on the streets—the most unforgiving of environments for an education.

During my own apprenticeship, I served as both instructor and pupil, sometimes simultaneously and usually unsuccessfully. Unfortunately for my prospective customers during this period, I didn't know a thing about value-based selling, solving business problems with my product or service, or listening to the customer. . . and it showed.

This inexperience, I suspect, is the reason CIOs roll their eyes when sales reps enter their office. Sadly, it's a stench so woven into our fabric I used to fear I could never rid myself of the smell, even after many years of success.

Like my peers at the time I graduated, I had the opportunity to take a cushy desk job making $35K to $40K a year, but I took the hard road and bet on myself. Throughout my first few years, I lost more than I won (by a wide margin) and made a whopping $19,000 (more or less) for my efforts.

Since I didn't have a base salary, I had to work hard and

learn fast. If I repeated mistakes, I paid the price. I obtained invaluable insights, experience and wisdom during those early years, and I wouldn't trade them for any price.

As salespeople, we're granted a seat at the CIO's conference table for a meeting they requested (or accepted). We're there to listen and maybe help. If the stars align, we'll be afforded an opportunity to continue the journey of earning the CIO's trust—and then their business.

Sales is a tough job. It takes a lot of no's to get to yes. But it's also an exciting job—one where we can impact business outcomes and create positive change for our customers. In this book, my co-author and I have gathered hard-won insights and advice from the people who make buying decisions to help you sell more, sell better and sell smarter.

Whether they like it or not, CIOs need us. They need us to be their business partners and educate them on what technologies can help drive their companies' success. Let's work hard to become the trusted advisors they seek and build meaningful, long-term relationships. Conduct yourself as a professional, and you'll be seen as one. You, your customers, and the profession deserve no less.

About the Authors

 David Silverstein has spent the last 25 years in technology sales and leadership. He is a results-driven relationship builder who is fiercely competitive and passionate about his career. He prides himself on building highly cooperative, energetic competitive cultures. Over his tenure he has held positions in direct and channel sales, target and strategic selling, and most recently VP of sales for a large publicly traded systems integrator.

 Randy Gaboriault has spent the last 15 years as an award-winning, global CIO across multiple industries, from aircraft engines and automotive to medical devices and health-care services. *CIO Magazine* editor-in-chief, Maryfran Johnson, named Randy an "exceedingly rare, triple threat CIO: a CIO that is equally talented at managing, problem-solving, and driving revenue." Randy has spent his career creating strategies for exceptional and differentiated technology-enabled value chains. With this experience has come thousands of interactions—good, bad, and ugly—with sales professionals and the sales apparatus of organizations large and small.

Acknowledgments

For a long time, I've dreamed of helping sales folks become better versions of ourselves by selling the right way instead of the annoying way. Now that vision has become reality in this book.

As with anything in life, I couldn't have achieved this goal without tons of insights and help from customers who have become friends. I leaned on my network of tech leaders with whom I have built lasting relationships over the years. They were kind enough to give of their time to make this book come alive.

My sincere thanks to my partner in this endeavor, Randy Gaboriault, a CIO, thought leader and lifelong friend whose stories about annoying salespeople first sparked the idea for this book.

Randy's advice and guidance over my 28 years in sales has been invaluable.

Special thanks to Chris Kohl and RJ Juliani, who provided plenty of content and guidance for us sales types to chew on. Chris and RJ were once prospects in my selling career. They have since become friends; without them this book would not exist.

Todd Forman and John Ford, you have been my therapy on days when I was ready to pack it in. You are amazing salespeople, and I thank you for sharing your stories and wisdom.

Thanks to Bill Morgan, John Dabek, Rajeev Nair, Bob Pick, Doug King, Kim Wismer, Michael Vennera, Sue Kozik, Steve Palmucci, whose perspectives and input helped to bring the book alive.

Thank you, Jennifer, for supporting and encouraging me

to get this book completed. You are my rock and make me smile. Mom and Adam, I love you and I appreciate you. Like my dad used to say, "If you want your prayers answered, get off your knees and hustle."

Finally, thank you, Carly and Gracie. You inspired me to finally finish something I started. I wanted to show you that anything is possible. If you want something, go get it and don't let anyone stand in the way.

I hope everyone can take one tidbit away from this book that will make them a better salesperson tomorrow.

Good selling!

Index

Made in United States
North Haven, CT
02 February 2023

31969715R00089